D1304079

ARMED WITH LOVE

STORIES OF THE DISCIPLES

ARMED WITH LOVE

STORIES OF THE DISCIPLES

Gerald N. Battle

Chapter decorations by Charles Cox

ABINGDON

Nashville

Library of Congress Cataloging in Publication Data

BATTLE, GERALD N. Armed with love. SUMMARY: Biographical profiles of the twelve disciples describing the influence of Christ's teachings on each of them. Bibliography: p. 1. Apostles—Juvenile literature. [1. Apostles] I. Title.

BS2440.B35   225.9′2 [B]   73-626

ISBN 0-687-01741-6

Manufactured by the Parthenon Press at Nashville, Tennessee, United States of America

To Mary

Contents

Before the Beginning

By any calculation it was a small band. There were only twelve of them. Only twelve men to attend the Master, to learn a whole new way of thinking, of living. Only this small group to listen, observe, learn, remember, and pass on to all the future generations of the world the most important message anyone would ever hear. The world in which they lived was small. For the most part they were Galileans. Probably very few of them had traveled outside Galilee except for occasional Passover pilgrimages to Jerusalem. Even the broader world of Palestine was not large. From Dan in the north to Beersheba in the south the distance was only about one hundred and fifty miles.

They were so few and from so small a world, and yet they took the story of Jesus and the truth of what he taught throughout the length and breadth of the Roman Empire and beyond! Always there were those who listened and believed. Always there were some who cared enough to take the message to others.

Who were these men? What were their backgrounds? How were they chosen? There are few facts which seem certain and sure. You will understand that the physical qualities and attitudes attributed to the disciples and other known characters such as Zebedee, father of James and John, are only the author's idea of how they may have looked, how they may have reacted. The aim is to show that appearance, physical ability, and even intellect varied among the twelve, as it must in any group of separate individuals.

These men were chosen by Jesus to work with him in a special way. In each Jesus saw the potential for something beyond anything any one of the twelve had ever dreamed for himself. Slowly, and sometimes painfully, each of the twelve—except for one—came into a new identity. Eleven of the twelve found themselves and added a new depth and a new dimension to their lives. The real tragedy of Judas is that, even though he knew Jesus, he was unable to transcend the limitations in which he bound himself. He alone of the twelve could not find himself.

Some things we do know. Certainly the one called Simon Peter seems to have been the leader of the group. He is always named first in the lists of the disciples. Simon Peter; his brother Andrew; the two sons of Zebedee, James and John; Matthew the tax collector, are those we know Jesus sought out first.

Later on, Jesus saw the need for others who could work with him in this special way. Perhaps he indicated, to the five first called, this need for others to help in the work. Twelve were chosen to represent the twelve tribes of Israel. It was a number rich in tradition and meaning. It could have been Simon Peter, often the first to speak, who asked, "Master, shall we bring others to you that you may select seven more to serve with us?" Jesus may have indicated that this was the way the remaining ones were to be chosen. Then, all of the five would think carefully about those friends they knew best who could be recommended. There could be no hasty decisions. Each man would be sure to recommend only those he felt certain could measure up. They knew the way ahead would not be easy.

10

We do not know, but perhaps it was Simon Peter who brought Philip to Jesus. Philip was from Bethsaida, as was Simon Peter. They may have known each other from boyhood. Surely Simon Peter, the leader, would have had some special friend to recommend. That friend might have been Philip. It could have been Andrew who sought out Thomas. Andrew was like Thomas—careful in his thought; thinking things through before acting. When Andrew learned from Jesus that others were needed, he may have thought of Thomas and brought him to Jesus. And so it might have happened with each of the five, considering others who might serve with them. Not all those recommended would be accepted by Jesus. And not all those selected would be men recommended by the five first chosen. There would be those who, having heard Jesus speak, would come to him and offer themselves, asking to be allowed to serve with him.

Perhaps as Jesus rested in some quiet place the disciples brought to him those they could recommend. Jesus might ask each one to sit down and talk with him. As they talked he might think to himself, "Ah, yes, here is one I can teach. Here is one who will surely help in this work I must do." To another he might say sadly, "There are other tasks for you to do. This is not your work." And so, at different times, in different places, the selection and choosing of the final twelve may have gone on. We cannot know. We can only guess and weave together out of the bits and pieces of history the stories of the disciples.

These stories are about unusual men, living in the greatest of all times. Each has his own story, for each was different from his fellows. We say they were unusual men—and so they were—but it was not wealth, social position, education, or intellect which set them apart. They were unusual because they had faith even when they were afraid. The big story is the coming together of the twelve and their relationships to Jesus. This, in the language of today, is what it is all about. Twelve men with nothing but their convictions, only their unconquerable faith in him, followed Jesus to Calvary. Had they stopped there we would have no story, but they followed beyond Calvary. There were fears, there were doubts, there were times of grave confusion, and there were mistakes; but the convictions remained, the faith continued. Soon there came the glorious understanding that they *could* go on, even though Jesus would not be physically with them. They *could* overcome their own fears, their own weaknesses, their own doubts. Together the twelve, with Matthias, Paul, and a few others, carried the good news to all people. Armed with love they set out to change the world—and they did.

ARMED WITH LOVE

STORIES OF THE DISCIPLES

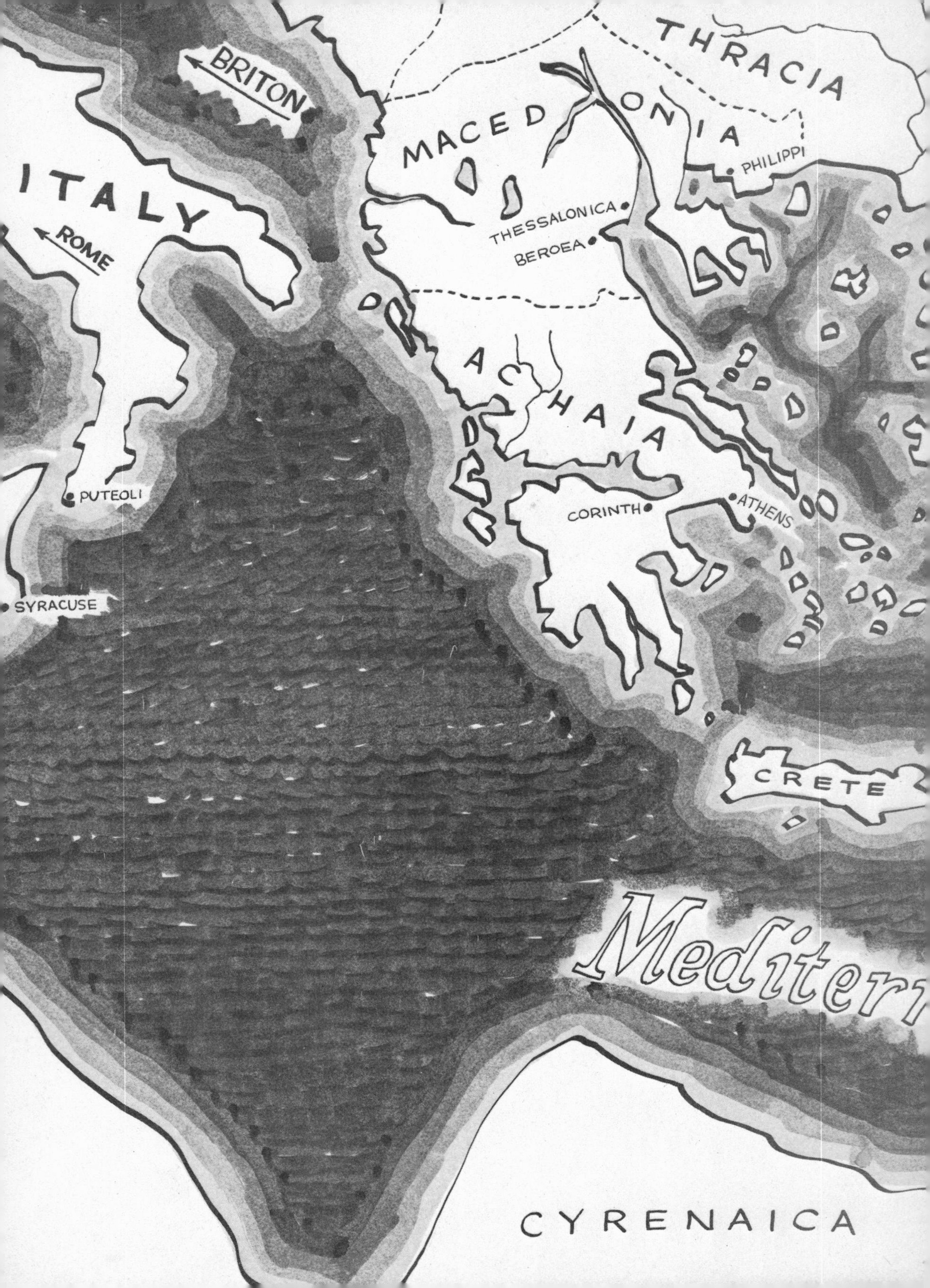
THRACIA
MACEDONIA
PHILIPPI
THESSALONICA
BEROEA
BRITON
ITALY
ROME
ACHAIA
CORINTH
ATHENS
PUTEOLI
SYRACUSE
CRETE
Mediterr
CYRENAICA

SCYTHIA
BITHYNIA
GALATIA
ALBANOPOLIS
PHRYGIA
KINGDOM of ARMENIA
CAPPADOCIA
ANTIOCH
HIEROPOLIS
LYSTRA
PERSIA
EDESSA
DERBE
REGNUM
CILICIA
PAMPHYLIA
LYCIA
RHODES
ANTIOCH
PARTHIA
SYRIA
CYPRUS
DAMASCUS
BABYLON
SIDON
CHALDEA'
TYRE
CANA
BETHSAIDA
GALILEE
CAPERNAUM
NAZARETH
NAIN
SAMARIA
PEREA
ARABIA
JUDEA
EPHRAIM
EMMAUS
JERICHO
JERUSALEM
BETHANY
BETHLEHEM
BETHPAGE
HEBRON
KERIOTH
INDIA
ETHIOPIA
EGYPT

ANDREW
The Man Who Was Never Alone

The long confinement in the shadowy darkness of my cell had sharpened my hearing. The sound outside was no louder than the scampering of rats, but I heard it clearly. Footsteps! These were not the heavy tread of my guards. Someone else was coming. Whoever it was took care to walk lightly.

As silently as my unknown visitor I edged to the door of the cell and pressed myself against the wall—listening. I was under sentence of death. When and how the sentence was to be carried out I had not been told. Could this be it? Was this my executioner come to do his work here in the cell? I pressed my back against the rough stone and prayed silently.

The footsteps stopped. I heard someone breathing just outside the door. The heavy bolt skittered in the lock. Slowly the cell door swung open. The dim light of a small lamp scattered the shadow. Dim as it was, the light blinded me.

"Andrew, Andrew!"

I knew that voice. Dropping my arm, I looked in the direction of the voice. Slowly my eyes adjusted to the unaccustomed light. It was Maximilla! Maximilla, the most faithful of all the small group who had listened to me preach the gospel of our Lord and learned to believe. But how could it be? The wife of the proconsul of Achaia in the cell of a man condemned to death by her husband!

"Maximilla, you should not be here. Egeus will be furious. You must know he has sentenced me to die. Don't test his anger further. Leave now, for your own safety." I could see her face clearly in the light of the lamp she held.

"Of course I know you are to die. That's why I'm here. The guard is a man I befriended once. Now he repays an old debt. I have a plan to save you. Let me tell it to you. There's plenty of time to talk before the guard changes again." Hurriedly Maximilla told me the plan. Her young, eager voice never rose above a whisper. I listened.

The plan was bold and dangerous. But still it might succeed. My heart beat more quickly. To breathe free air again—only a man in prison knows the longing. And then I knew the plan was not for me. My face betrayed me.

"Why do you look so strange?" Maximilla asked, forgetting to keep her voice low.

I smiled. "There's a story I've never told in Achaia. Is there time for me to tell it now?" Maximilla nodded.

"Sit down and listen," I told her. "You've heard me preach of the words of our Lord Jesus Christ, but you have never heard my own story, how it all began for a fisherman named Andrew. I'll tell it to you now.

"It all began there near the shores of our blue sea in Galilee."
I fell to remembering back to the very beginning.

"Andrew, Andrew," my brother called me though I was still
some distance down the shore from him. The deep, impatient voice
would not be denied and I quickened my pace, taking care not to
stumble among the rocks. My sandals were nearly worn through
from the journey. Simon met me as I hurried toward him.

"You've been gone so long—three days now it has been. Have
you forgotten we are fishermen? Our customers expect fresh fish
for their table!" As always the words came from Simon in a rush.

"You should have been with us, brother," I replied. "John and
I went to hear John the Baptizer—the son of Zacharias. He is a
man to hear! At first we thought surely he must be the Messias,
but it was not so. On the day we were to return he looked over our
heads at one behind us in the crowd. The Baptizer said, 'Behold
the lamb of God.' We turned, and it was to one called Jesus he
pointed. John and I left the Baptizer and followed after Jesus.
We spoke with him at some length. Simon, I am sure I have found
the Messias! He is Jesus of Nazareth! There is something about
him, some quality I cannot explain." I almost shouted the words.
I had spoken so certainly and with such confidence even Simon
was impressed. He was inclined to question any news I might bring.

"You seem so certain, Andrew. How can you be sure?"

"Oh, Simon, you would have been sure if you had seen him and
spoken to him. He is truly the Messias! Let me take you to him."
If only Simon would listen. I knew I could not be mistaken.

"There will be time enough for that. We still have our business
to attend to. While you and John have been off listening to this
John the Baptizer fellow preaching in the desert, James and I have
been seeing that the boats were overhauled and the nets mended.
We go fishing this night. You'd better rest a bit and get something

to eat. Where is John? Why did you come back alone?" asked Simon.

"I hurried on ahead. I knew you'd be impatient, and besides I wanted to bring you the good news. Look, here comes John now." I pointed down the shore where I could see John coming toward us. Simon merely nodded and motioned me to go on to the house and rest while he waited to greet John.

Lois, Simon's wife, greeted me warmly at the house and offered food, but I was not hungry. I lay down to sleep, but sleep came slowly, for my thoughts were all of what I had heard and seen. When would I see the one called Jesus again? How could I convince my brother to let me take him to meet Jesus? Would Simon believe as I did? Simon was our leader—even James listened to him. If Simon were convinced that Jesus was truly the Messias, others would follow. My brother was a stubborn fellow and impulsive as well. Sometimes he spoke before he really thought, but when convinced he never turned back. John had been there with me. John was as certain as I. If only Simon and James would listen to us. I tossed on my bed as the thoughts tumbled through my mind. Finally sleep came, as it always does when weariness refuses to let go.

The pleasant smell of cooking food woke me from my sleep. Lois' laughing eyes mocked me as I rubbed the sleep from mine. If I had no thought of food before, now I was famished. Simon joined me at the table, poking a finger in my ribs. "We'll need a good catch tonight just to feed my brother, wife! I'm half a head taller and twice as broad, but look at the way he eats!" My brother Simon was in a merry mood. It was always this way with Simon when we were nearing the time to go out on the sea with the nets. He loved the challenge of the sea and to test his strength against the long night's work. He was right. He *was* half a head taller than I and more heavily muscled. There were only a few years between us, but Simon had been as large at thirteen as I was now at twenty-two. Simon at twenty-five was a giant of a man and the best fisherman in Galilee. He loved fishing. With me it was an honest livelihood—no more. We had always been fishermen. My father, Jonah, his father before him—all had cast their nets in the Sea of Galilee. It was the same with James and John. Their father, Zebedee, and his father before him had been fishermen. We were all fishermen. We always *would* be fishermen. It was a good living, and even though the work was hard, we had more than many of our neighbors. The partnership with Zebedee had been profitable for both our families. And yet I had dreamed a dream for all those years— a secret dream, of course. For foolish dreams are best kept secret, and my dream was a very foolish one. As boys we had all been sent to the synagogue school. John and I were the same age—a few years younger than James and Simon. Both of us were better students than our brothers. James was much like Simon, a fisherman who loved the sea, but no match for my brother in strength.

The school was a whole new world for me and I loved the learning I received. Simon was impatient to be done with it, thinking only of the day when he could take a place in the boat. With me it was different. I wished there would be no end to school. Secretly I dreamed of the Scribal College in Jerusalem. That was what I wanted, but it could only be a dream. When I was old enough, I took my place in one of the boats. Soon after, our father died, and shortly after that, Simon married. Simon had his own house and I looked after our mother. There was no time for foolish dreaming. The boats demanded all our time.

When our mother died Simon asked me to come and live in his home, and so I did. Had I left the fishing business it would have meant hiring someone to take my place. It seemed too costly an expense. I dreamed my dreams and kept them to myself. Once in a great while, I allowed myself a small break in the routine of fishing. It was on such an occasion I had persuaded John to go with me, to hear the one called John the Baptizer.

21

When I told Simon I wanted to go south to Judea to hear John the Baptizer, he couldn't understand it. "They say the man is mad. He lives on nuts and berries, and wears animal skins, I've been told. I've heard the stories people tell about him. Go, if you must, but we can spare you for only a few days. Since you've persuaded John to go with you, the rest of us will mend the nets and sails and recaulk the boats while you are gone. James and I and the crewmen will have enough to do, and the equipment needs overhauling. Don't stay away too long." My brother shook his head and turned back to the boats. I hurried off in search of John, eager to be on our way.

All these things were in my mind as I ate. I would have thought about it more, but Simon was eager to get to the shore and do some casting before we took the boats out. I had had my holiday from fishing. I sighed and hurried after him. While Simon used the casting net, I busied myself about the boat, checking it carefully for the long night ahead. A short distance down the shore James and John finished some last-minute repairs on the big drift net spread along the shore. My tasks finished, I watched my brother whirl the casting net and let it fall. For all his bigness and seeming roughness, my brother was a gentle man. You could see it in the way he handled the net. His great hands let the net fall slowly, unfolding like a giant bubble. He made his cast so lightly the net rode on the surface of the water for an instant. Simon was having no luck with the casting net. I hoped it was not an omen of the fishing luck to come. We'd need full nets to make up for the fishing we had not done these past three days. For some reason, why I do not know, my gaze turned away from the sea and wandered to the road behind. The figure coming toward me seemed vaguely familiar. Something in the spring of the walk, the long rhythmic stride, stirred my memory. Whoever came was yet too far away for me to make out the face, but there was something I seemed to recognize. My gaze turned back to the sea. Simon shook out his net and folded it with his usual care. If we caught fish tonight, we would have to catch them in the drift net. My brother's usual good fortune had snared no fish with the casting net.

I had heard no footsteps, so the sudden voice startled me as I sat there on the shore watching Simon put away his casting net. The voice came from behind and said, "Follow me, and I will make you fishers of men." That voice—even before I turned I knew it was Jesus who spoke! He stood just behind me, smiling and with his hands outstretched. There were a thousand things I had to say, but the words wedged in my throat and I spoke none of them.

I sat there mute as any stone, gazing at Jesus as he turned and walked on down the shore. Shaking the bewilderment from my head, I turned back to Simon. My brother walked past me, following after Jesus. He had the look on his face he wore in moments of great stress. It was the same look I had seen when he fought a sudden storm to keep our boat from turning broadside to the waves.

I got to my feet and hurried after them. My brother's words tossed back at me brought me to a halt. "Andrew, go to the house. Tell Lois we'll have a guest tonight, and then come after us."

Simon was right, of course. Jesus would be tired. He'd need a place to stay. Perhaps he would accept my bed! I gave one long look after them, and saw Simon catch up with Jesus. They both walked on down the shore where James and John were mending the drift net. I hurried to the house. When I explained to Lois we would have a guest, she was upset. Her mother was ill and required all her attention. How could she prepare a meal? I left her and hurried back to join the others.

Jesus leaned against the boat drawn up on the shore. Seated at his feet, James, John, and Simon listened while he talked. Silently I took my seat beside my brother. How long we listened as Jesus talked, I do not know. I remember the night grew chill and I kindled a small fire there on the shore. At last I could not help but notice how tired Jesus seemed to be. "Sir, will you not rest with us in my brother's house? Surely you must be very weary, for we have kept you so late, talking to us here. My brother's wife has prepared food for a meal." I hesitated to say more, knowing Simon himself would wish to offer the hospitality of his house.

Jesus smiled at me, but before he could answer, Simon was on his feet and speaking. "Come, good Rabbi, share my home with me. Andrew is right—we've kept you talking too long." Taking Jesus by the arm he urged him toward the road. Together the three of us walked to Simon's house. James and John stayed to secure the boats and put away the drift net. There had been no thought of fishing after Jesus came.

My heart was full of happiness. Jesus had said, "Follow me, and I will make you fishers of men." I had no doubt that he would explain his words more fully, but my mind was already made up. No matter where he led, I would follow him. I only hoped Simon would be there as well. How quickly Jesus had singled Simon out. They had not exchanged a word before, and yet Jesus had chosen him. They walked ahead, my brother's arm around Jesus. What a happy night this was! I ran past them to the house.

At the house I quickly placed fresh coverings on my bed. I cautioned Lois to be sure the children did not make noises and disturb our guest. Taking my warmest cloak, I climbed the outside steps to the roof. Wrapping my cloak about me, I lay down and slept.

The days that followed were days of learning, watching, and listening. Old Zebedee was not happy to see his sons and Simon and me walking and talking with Jesus instead of attending to the fishing business. The old man grumbled and complained, but nevertheless he hired men to take our places. Salome, his wife, encouraged James and John to follow Jesus and cautioned Zebedee to hold his tongue.

I well recall the first time I heard Jesus speak in the synagogue. The elders were amazed, and not all of them were pleased, at what he said. Jesus gave no lofty exposition of the law, with careful legal point piled on careful point. He spoke to them saying he had come to preach the gospel of the Lord to all men, the poor, the bewildered, and the confused. There was a man who was disturbed in his mind, and he shouted out in a loud voice telling Jesus to leave him alone. The man was shouting and throwing himself on the floor. Jesus spoke to him quietly, and in a moment the man was clear in his mind and sitting peacefully on the bench, listening to the words that Jesus spoke.

As we left the synagogue, many of the elders talked among themselves and wondered who this rabbi was who spoke so plainly of doing God's will. They wondered how he could heal a man by merely speaking to him. So we left the synagogue and returned to Simon's house. Lois was much distressed because her mother had become more ill in our absence. Her mother's fever was very high. As soon as Jesus learned of the sick woman, he went to her and lifted her hand. Immediately the fever left her and she was well again.

Twice now I had seen Jesus perform miracles of healing, and there were many more to come. At first I could not understand why he always cautioned those he healed not to go about praising him or telling others of what he had done for them. Gradually I began to understand. Jesus' compassion for all who suffered made him want to help all those he could reach, but he did not want to become known as a miracle worker only. His real mission was to teach people the word of God and how to live with each other. This was a truth I learned and never forgot.

Once Jesus went away from us for a little while in Capernaum, indicating he had business he wished to conduct alone. The four of us waited for him at Simon's house. In the afternoon Jesus came, telling us about Levi, one of the tax collectors we knew too well. When Jesus told us he had chosen Levi to work with him as one of us, we were surprised. Levi was honest in his collections, but he took his silver from the Romans. Most of us had little love for

Jews who worked for Roman pay. Still, even in the short time we had known Jesus, we had learned something. I saw James and Simon choke back the hot words I knew were on the tip of their tongues. Later, when the tax collector himself came to invite us to his home, Simon's face flushed red when he greeted Levi, but his words were not unkind. James's greeting was short but sincere enough. John and I gave Levi a hearty welcome. Younger brothers seem to accept surprise more easily than their elders.

"I'm giving a dinner tonight and inviting my old friends. It will be a farewell to my former life. You'll be my guest with the Master? I beg to have the honor of your presence." Levi spoke to Jesus, but his look included all of us.

"We accept your invitation, Levi. All of us will be there," replied Jesus. Levi smiled and hurried home to prepare for his dinner. This time my brother could not hold back the words which sprang to his lips. "Master, we do not know the guests who will sit at Levi's table. You may be sure they are no friends of ours. We have no business there. Let me go after him and tell him we cannot attend."

"Simon's right. A tax collector's friends are no friends of ours," said James.

"Levi is one of us. I have given him a new name—Matthew. None are excluded from God's love. If you follow me, you go where I go. I'll sup at Matthew's house this night." Having said these words, Jesus retired from us to be alone and meditate and pray, as was his custom. Simon and James looked at each other, but they did not say another word.

And so we dined with Matthew and his friends. Our newest disciple set a costly table and we ate well. The guests were strange indeed to most of us. Some were minor officials of the government; others, those who dealt in various goods and knew the tax collector well. I noticed Jesus mingled with the guests and greeted all of them, speaking to first one and then another. Matthew was very pleased with the honor Jesus paid him by his presence. Even Simon regained his good humor and complimented Matthew on the supper. It was the last such table we were to sit before for many a day.

The next day we went through Galilee, and Jesus stopped often to speak to the people and teach them the truths he had made known to us. Gradually there were others who became a part of our company. Simon brought Philip to Jesus. We had grown up with Philip in Bethsaida and knew him well for the true man he was. It was Philip who asked Bartholomew, sometimes called Nathanael, to come and meet with Jesus.

I myself asked Thomas to come and talk to Jesus. We had been friends since boyhood, Thomas and I. John, Philip, Thomas, and I were all of the same age. Thomas was a faithful man, and I was happy Jesus chose him to be one of us.

There was a time when our band was almost complete—for Jesus had told us he would choose only twelve—and there on Mount Tabor, Jesus called me to his side. He asked me if I had seen Judas of Kerioth among the crowd who followed us. It was I who Judas had asked, some days ago, for a chance to talk with Jesus. I had passed his request on to my brother Simon, but Simon had said no. If Jesus wanted to talk with Judas, he would make his wishes known. Now Jesus must have noticed Judas in the crowd and decided to talk with him. He had been pleased to learn Jesus asked for him. I watched him as he talked with Jesus. I do not know what they said, but he became our twelfth disciple. Though Simon never trusted him completely, I thought Judas was a good man and a true friend of Jesus. I was as sure of Judas as any man I ever knew, and I was wrong in my judgment. I never forgot I was the first one of the twelve of us to call Judas friend. I was the one who helped to bring him to the attention of Jesus. If only I had judged him more carefully! And yet I learned to pity him, though I could never forgive myself.

Still the crowds followed Jesus. They were so great we took a boat and went across the Sea of Galilee to the north shore. There we went into the desert country a little way, but still the people came. As always Jesus would stop and speak to them, no matter how late in the day or how weary he might be. This day he realized the time was late and the people would be hungry before they could reach their homes. We must provide the people food, he told us. Philip, looking at the crowd, said, "Master, two hundred denarii will not buy bread enough for each one to have even a little. There is no place here where we might buy bread in any case." Then Jesus asked us to see if any in the crowd had brought some food. I remembered seeing a small lad with a parcel of food. I looked for him and brought him to the Master.

Five small loaves and three fishes were all the boy had. He placed his parcel in Jesus' hands. Then Jesus thanked him and asked him if he would share his food. The boy nodded his head and I led him back to his place. Jesus told us to divide the people into groups of fifty. When we had done this, we passed among them, breaking from the loaves and fishes some for each person. With only five small loaves and three fishes we had enough to feed them all. Whenever we broke off a piece, somehow there remained enough for the next person, and so it went. The crowd did not realize how the food was provided, but I marveled to myself at Jesus' concern for the people even in small things. I had seen him heal Simon's wife's mother, make blind people see, and even cure lepers, but this was a different kind of miracle.

One of the greatest days was when we twelve were alone with Jesus near the town of Caesarea Philippi. Jesus had gone off to pray alone. The twelve of us sat together talking among ourselves when he came back to us. "Who do men say I am?" he asked. One of us—I do not remember which one it was—said, "Some say you are John the Baptizer; others say you are Elias or Jeremias, or one of the prophets."

"And who do *you* say I am?" Jesus asked us. We looked at one another, each hesitating to be the first to speak. Then I heard my brother's voice speak out, "You are the Christ, the Son of the living God!"

"Blessed are you, Simon-bar-Jonah, for no man has revealed this to you, but my Father in heaven. And I say to you, that you are Peter, and upon this rock I will build my church, and the gates of hell will not stand against it." With these words Jesus gave my brother a new name, Peter—Simon Peter. Of all of us who had come to know Jesus, listened to him, learned from him, watched him work and heard him teach, only Simon, now Simon Peter, had understood who he was. I was happy just to be one of those around Jesus, for I knew my talents were small. But my brother, Simon Peter, the rock of Galilee, had realized more clearly than the rest of us who Jesus really was. I could not keep from reaching out and touching Simon Peter on the shoulder. He turned and put his hand on mine. I was glad we were brothers.

The days were so full and rushed so swiftly by it is hard to recall them now at all. There was that happy day when we marched into Jerusalem and the people shouted and waved palm branches. How gay we all were that day! Judas, especially, was happy. His face shone, and even though he seldom smiled, that day he smiled. It was on that same day Philip brought the group of young Greeks to me. They wished to speak with Jesus and had come to Philip because they knew he spoke their language. Philip's mother was Greek, and he spoke Greek better than the rest of us. Philip came to me saying the young Greeks had journeyed far and wanted to speak with Jesus. Usually I spoke with Simon Peter before bringing people to the Master, but my brother was on some errand, so I went directly to Jesus. He told me to bring the visitors to him and I did.

I left them talking to Jesus and went off a little way apart. For an hour Jesus talked with them. I saw how earnest they were in their speech and how they hung on every word Jesus said to them. Finally he bade them good-bye and, courteously, they came to me before they left, to thank me for taking them to Jesus. Little did I think then, when I spoke to them so haltingly—for I had little Greek—one day I would learn to speak their language as easily as my own. I never dreamed one day I would live and work in the Greek Islands. How long ago that seems now.

Looking back, I see that Jesus tried to prepare us for the day when he would no longer be with us. Yet, though he tried to tell us more than once, I could not understand it then. Perhaps it was not so much that I *could not* understand, but rather that I put it from my mind, refusing to face up to what he said. In those days life without Jesus could only seem no life at all. I had not yet learned my lessons well, but there were other days of learning yet to come.

It was at the time of the Passover, and we were in Jerusalem for the holiest time of the year. I smiled to myself as I thought of the long-forgotten dream of attending the Scribal College in Jerusalem. How glad I was my dream had not come true. To work with Jesus was a dream I had not known how to dream. Yet it had come true—the greatest dream of all.

John and Simon Peter were selected by Jesus to go and prepare a room and make arrangements for the feast of Passover. When John was chosen, I thought perhaps I might be asked to go with him. John and I were ever in each other's company when Jesus did not require him. But I was not to be the choice, and Simon Peter was assigned to go with John. James and I watched the bustling throng and heard the muttered threats of those who did not like to see the crowds which always followed Jesus. Still, we knew our Master's powers and had no fear, in spite of all the warnings he had given us. We were simple-minded men who could not comprehend the treachery surrounding us in Jerusalem.

That night we gathered in the upper room of the house where John and Simon Peter had made arrangements for the Passover meal. We all reclined about the table. John sat next to Jesus, as he

30

nearly always did. For a moment I wished I might sit next to Jesus once, but quickly I put the wish from my heart and listened as Jesus spoke to us.

"I wanted to eat this Passover feast with you before the time comes when I must leave you," he said. "My time of suffering comes soon. I will not drink of the fruit of the vine until the kingdom of God shall come. Take this cup and divide it among you." Jesus passed the cup among us and each of us drank from it. Then he broke some bread and passed it among us saying, "This is my body which is given for you: this do in remembrance of me."

I did not fully understand what Jesus said. Later I would ask John to explain it to me. John always seemed to understand Jesus more clearly than I ever did. Often he explained to Philip and me things we did not wholly understand. Jesus continued to speak to us. Sometimes his voice dropped so low I could not always hear. I knew he was reminding us of his teachings. He said we must be faithful to those teachings and carry out the work he had assigned us to do.

Gradually the hour grew late and we prepared to leave for the Garden of Gethsemane, the place Jesus had chosen to pray and meditate. Judas had left earlier, so we were only eleven to walk the short distance from the house to Gethsemane with our Master. Pulling our cloaks about us, we left the house. It was not really cold. The day had been warmer than usual. Yet somehow the air was chill. We walked along our way with one another. Some strange sadness lay on each of us, and our talk was in low tones. I noticed my brother Simon Peter spoke not a word, nor did John. Something weighed heavily on their minds.

When we reached the garden, Jesus went a little way apart from us. Simon Peter, John, and James went with him, and he talked with them. Soon Jesus drew apart from them to be alone. The rest of us stayed together, huddled in our cloaks. We slept. Twice I stirred in my sleep. I thought I heard voices, but before I came fully awake, I slept again. At last I awoke and heard voices. I flung off my cloak and stood up. A group with lighted torches came toward us. In the flare of the torchlight, metal helmets shone. These were armed men led by an officer! My heart beat faster. Now all of us were awake.

I was nearest to the group of soldiers, with Philip at my side and Thomas close to me. The three of us drew back. Jesus came with Simon Peter at his side and, just behind my brother, James and John. Then my eyes could not believe what they saw, but it was true. Judas stepped forward and pointed to Jesus! An order was given. One of the men stepped forward to lay hands on Jesus. My brother pulled his sword and swung at the man. I saw the man stagger backward, bleeding, his hand clasped to his head. Other soldiers quickly surged forward, and I heard Jesus' calm voice telling my brother to put down his sword.

I did not know what to do. Surely they would take us all to prison. Something even worse might happen. I ran! Those nearest to me scattered. Like chickens when a storm approaches, we ran in all directions.

I do not know what others did. I followed no path but ran straight down the hillside, dodging olive trees in the darkness. I stumbled and fell often in my flight. When I fell I got up and ran again until I could run no more. My knees were cut and bleeding and my legs bruised in a dozen places. My cloak was torn. I stopped because I could run no farther. My breath came in great gasps. I was afraid, and very much alone. I saw no one else and heard no footsteps. Slowly my reason came back to me.

Why had I run? Who wanted Andrew, one of the least of the twelve followers of Jesus? It was not *me* they wanted—not any of us. It was only Jesus of whom they were afraid. But why had Judas led them to Jesus? He was one of us! I could breathe more easily now, but there was much I could not understand. Only one thing was clear to me. I had been chosen by Jesus to work with him, to be one of his chosen twelve. I had deserted him! I had run, like a person who did not even know him. While my brother drew his sword and defended Jesus, I had taken to my heels.

Before, I had been hot with fear. Now I was calm. I felt as cold as the snow upon Mount Hermon's top. I was still afraid, but my fear was not of the high priest's soldiers, not even fear of Caiaphas, the high priest. I was afraid of myself. I had not stood my ground. I knew the others near me had fallen back at first. Now they were probably with Jesus in a prison cell. Only I would not be there. Only I, and Judas who had betrayed him, would be absent. They would think I had been partner to the treachery! What else could they think? And they would be wrong, and yet so near to being right. I had not betrayed Jesus, but I had forsaken him. Now I could not go back.

I stood up and looked around. The darkness was deeper now. The first half-light of dawn was still an hour away. My eyes, accustomed now to darkness, could see more clearly. I found a road and followed it. I did not know where it led. It did not really matter. All that mattered I had left behind. And so it was I walked that road. Dawn came; I hardly noticed. The sun grew brighter overhead, and still I walked. Now and then some traveler came toward me on the road. They always turned to stare at me. I was conscious of their stares, but I never looked back at them or spoke.

I had stopped thinking and my legs behaved as if they were not mine. Somehow, one foot stepped forward and was followed by the other. It was no conscious will of mine which made them walk, or guided them. At last the heat of the day made me realize I was very thirsty. I could see a village in the distance, and yet some way off. There would be water there. I tried to walk more quickly and I could not. I looked down at my feet. My sandals were broken, my feet torn and bleeding. Suddenly I was tired. I must have been walking for many hours.

At last I stumbled into the village. There was a well. A small girl, the age of Simon Peter's daughter, filled a water jar at the well. I asked her for a drink. She held out her water jar to me and I drank my fill. I thanked the child and limped over to a nearby tree. I slumped beneath it, too tired to move. I felt I could never again lie quietly and sleep. Tired as I was, I felt there could be no sleep for me. I had too many thoughts to carry in my head. The stinging sorrow of my own weakness would never let me rest. Still, sleep *did* come. I slept beneath the tree. Hours later I awoke, somewhat refreshed but so sore I could not move without crying out. It was almost evening. I was still dull-witted from my deep sleep. Slowly I recalled the previous night, and my sorrow came rushing back to me.

There was only one thing to do. I must return to Jerusalem! With great difficulty I got to my feet. I took out my old, dull knife and cut a branch from the tree under which I had slept. I'd need a staff to walk the long road back to Jerusalem. I moved slowly, leaning on the tree limb I had cut. My steps were slow, but I was thinking more clearly now. The sky was turning black. In moments night would fall, but I was headed toward Jerusalem. I would rejoin Jesus and the others! I felt a happiness I had not known before. I had seen our Master perform miracles. Never once had a miracle happened to me. I felt one happening to me now. My heart thumped stronger in my chest. My feet felt light enough to dance. I flung aside the staff that I had cut. "I am coming. Wait for me, I'm coming!" The words flew out of my mouth in a loud shout. The women filling water jars at the well looked up and stared at me.

A dusty figure in torn cloak and broken sandals, running down the road, shouting to the wind—how strange I must have seemed to them. They must have looked at one another and whispered "Madman" to themselves. And they were right. I was mad with both sadness and joy. Sad because of all that had happened; full

34

of joy at the thought of seeing Jesus again, no matter what danger lay ahead. Too soon my miracle vanished. One minute I was running. The next minute I lay sprawling unconscious in the dust.

When I awoke I lay on a bed in the corner of a house. A figure bent over me and placed a cool cloth on my forehead. I tried to speak. Only a croak came from my throat. The woman who tended me smiled and told me not to speak. She brought me a bowl of barley soup and fed it to me slowly. I hadn't realized how hungry I was. I ate a little and then went back to sleep again. The good woman and her husband looked after me until I was strong enough to go. I had only my thanks to give them, and they wanted nothing more. Rosh—that was the husband's name—had found me unconscious in the road as he returned home from his fields. He had brought me on his back to his own house and tended me.

I said farewell and thanked them once again and hurried toward Jersualem. Late evening found me in the city. Where should I start to look? I would go first to the house where we had eaten the Passover meal. Our friend who had let us use his upper room might have some word. I ran down narrow, crowded streets until I found the house. Impatiently I knocked. The owner of the house appeared and seemed to expect me.

"Your friends are gathered in the room above," he said. Without a word I ran past him up the stairs. Simon Peter, John, Matthew, James, Bartholomew, Philip, Simon Zelotes, Thaddaeus, James-the-Less were there. My brother came to greet me, and close behind him, John. They took me aside and told me all that had happened. Jesus was gone! Crucified! And yet he had risen again! I was prepared for prison—even to die with him. But he had died alone, and I had run away! I heard the words but I could not give them to my mind to see. Suddenly I realized Simon Peter was weeping. I had never seen my brother weep before, and now he could not hold back the tears as he told me of his denial of our Master.

He held nothing back, and the bitter words with which he spoke of his own weakness were like whips upon his back.

"Three times I denied our Lord! Three times I turned my back on him. How can you call me brother, Andrew? And yet, if I could have another chance to die for him, I know I would not falter." My brother dropped his head into his hands. I looked at Simon Peter and I never loved my brother more than at that moment. Slowly I began my own story. I told how I had fled headlong from Jerusalem and my decision to return, and then the illness which had caused my delay.

"I too would die for him. It costs too much to run away. I'll not do that again." The words came slowly and I knew what I said was true. I would *not* run away again. My brother threw his arms about me and we held each other close.

"We must all live for him, if we can," said John. "Only if we live will we be able to carry on his work. We'll need each other— as we always have—now more than ever."

Simon Peter seemed to take heart from John's words. He put aside his grief and stood up, drawing himself to his full height. Then he spoke to us all. "Come, let us eat together. Then we will plan on how we are to be about the Master's work. Somehow I feel he will direct us in the way our feet must go. First let us eat." My brother sat down at the table and all the rest of us gathered with him there.

As we ate and talked among ourselves, I sat between John and Simon Peter. I noticed John turn and look behind him, and then my brother turned to look. Curious at what attracted them, I also turned. Jesus stood there in our midst, and suddenly all of us saw him!

"Peace be with you all," he said. We were so full of awe we could not answer him. He showed his hands to us and turned to let us see his side. At last we found our tongues, and all of us broke into

36

speech. Each of us, in his own words, expressed the joy we felt at seeing him again.

"Peace to you all," he said again. "As my Father has sent me, so I send you." Jesus spoke these words to us and more. Some of us asked questions and he answered us. We would have pressed him for more answers to our questions but, as suddenly as he had appeared, he vanished from us.

"Later we saw him again on the shore of the Sea of Galilee," I continued. "It was here he charged each one of us to go into all the world and preach the gospel to every creature. He said he would be with us always, even to the end of the world. This is what I believe, Maximilla. Now you see why I cannot try your plan. It would be running away again. 'I will be with you always, even to the end of the world.' That's what Jesus said. You must learn to believe these words as I do. This is what gives me the courage to conquer my own fears.

"There were so many times I knew fear. As a fisherman, storms at sea frightened me many times. There we were only men throwing our bodies against the wind. When I really came to know Jesus, all that was changed. I am still Andrew—only a man. A part of me longs to fly this prison, risk anything no matter how desperate the chance. But there is another part which says, stay and suffer just a little while—he is with you always. So I *must* stay. If I stay—even though Egeus, your husband the proconsul, puts me to death—you and the others who have listened to me can believe as I do."

Maximilla wept softly. It grieved me to see her so distressed. There was nothing more we could say to each other. I had said all I knew to say. If only she could believe. She spoke no word but only grasped my hand and, clutching her lamp, stumbled through the open doorway of my cell. Somehow I felt she understood.

37

Moments later the guard came, slammed the cell door and slid home the bolt.

"No nails, Andrew," Egeus said. "The leather thongs will bind you to the cross and let you die more slowly." I saw him smile his cunning smile as he tested the thongs to make sure they held secure. He spoke again.

"You should have stayed in Galilee, Galilean. You had no need to come to Achaia to preach about your Jesus. Look at them now, the ones who listened to your preaching. They come to watch you die without a word in your behalf.

"Even my wife, Maximilla, does not plead for your life. I'd have wagered all I own she'd be here begging mercy for you on her knees. You cast your spell on her once, Christian; no more. See how quietly she watches with the others. All she asked me for was a bit of ground to lay you in when you are dead."

Egeus tugged at my thongs once more. He turned and, followed by his officers, strode off. I saw him pause where Maximilla knelt and look down at her. Fighting against the blackness coming over me, I could barely hear the words he spoke to her.

"You'll not have long to wait, my wife. Another hour and you can bury him." Egeus walked away.

Maximilla looked across at Andrew hanging on the strange X-shaped cross. He was past making any sound. His eyes were closed, and there was the faint trace of a smile on his face. Perhaps he was already dead. Maximilla knew she had been right not to plead with her husband for Andrew's life. She would bury him and send word to his brother. Andrew did not run away—that would be her message. It was the message he would have wanted sent. Maximilla looked around her. They were mostly women in

38

the group, perhaps a half dozen men among them. Together they would remember what Andrew had taught them. They would remember that so long as they believed, they would never be alone. If she could remember no more than that it would be enough. With his own death Andrew had taught them how to live. Slowly she stood up and walked toward the cross.

JOHN
The Man Who Learned to Understand

This was the part of the work he disliked most—not that he really **liked any part** of fishing. The net was still wet and the heavy cords tore at his hands. John held the net-mender's tool in his hand and rested for a minute. It was an odd-shaped tool some seven inches long and made of iron. One end was flattened, and a hole a little larger than the heavy cords used for the net had been drilled in the flat part of the end. From the circular flat part of the tool a slender column about an inch long ran to a three-sided shaft which continued several inches to become a round shaft tapered to a point. This was the net-mender's tool. It had no proper name, but Galilean fishermen had used the tool for many years, calling it only the net-mender's tool.

John again began to work on the net. He sat in the boat drawn up on the shore, opposite his brother James. The heavy drift net spilled out of the boat and on the rocky shore. His hands were rubbed red and raw from his work. The net had suffered a large tear and they had been working to mend it for some hours. Each broken cord had to be carefully unraveled back to an anchor knot. Here the broken ends were cut away and a fresh cord carefully secured and tied in place. The mesh had to be replaced exactly to measure so there would be no weakening of the net. The job was long and tedious. John was impatient to be done with it. Even though he had no love for the boats, fishing was better than mending nets. Anything was better than this tedious work! He jabbed at a knot with the sharp end of his net-mender's tool. The point glanced off the water-hardened knot and cut the flesh of his palm.

"Owwh!" he exclaimed in pain and flung the iron tool carelessly across the boat, narrowly missing the foot of his brother.

"That temper of yours is going to win you a thrashing one of these days," said James. "You'd be getting it now if that point had come an inch closer."

"I tell you this is no life for me," replied John, holding his cut hand with the other and scowling. "I'm sorry I threw down the tool. I had no wish to injure you. I only wanted to get the clumsy thing out of my hand."

"Best get back to work, brother. Our father expects us to finish mending this net in time to take the boat out this evening. He'll have sharp words for us if we don't finish it in time." James handed the tool back to John.

"No matter what we do he has sharp words for us! He's never satisfied these days," said John, taking the tool and resuming his mending.

The two brothers worked on in silence for a while. Zebedee, the father of James and John, was the owner of a fishing fleet and a prosperous businessman, but he required his sons to work as hard as any of his hired men. Simon and Andrew, their neighbors, owned a share in the business, but they too knew Zebedee's sharp tongue and quick temper. Zebedee insisted that the owners of a business had to work harder than anyone else.

"How hard will the hired men work if those who benefit most do not toil?" he asked. For Simon and James the hard work was no problem. They loved fishing and the sea. They cared little for Zebedee's sharp and often sarcastic tongue, and shrugged off the older man's remarks. Andrew, Simon's younger brother, did not share his brother's passion for the boats, but Andrew did his job and held his tongue. John was the one who was openly resentful. His quick temper kept him in continual trouble with his father.

Now as John worked on the net his sore hand served as a constant reminder of his dislike for the job. He looked over at his older brother. James was so different from John it was hard to believe they were brothers. John was tall and thin. James was shorter and very broad of shoulder. Among the fishermen of Galilee only Simon-bar-Jonah was more powerful and more skillful in handling nets and boats. James had a temper, and he showed it when aroused, but it was not kept on so short a leash as John's. Of the two John was the thinker and James was the doer. But though they were different there was a real affection between the two young men. They were like their constant companions and longtime neighbors in this respect. Simon and Andrew were very close to each other, and so were James and John.

All these things passed through John's mind as he worked on the net. He raised his eyes for a moment and looked down the shore. He was surprised to see three men approaching. The first he did not recognize, but surely the two following were Simon and Andrew. He wondered if there was some trouble and stood up in the boat for a better look. James turned to see what had attracted his brother's attention. Now the stranger was standing beside the boat, looking straight into John's eyes.

42

"Follow me," he said and stood there, holding John's eyes with his own steady gaze.

"You are the one called Jesus! I saw you baptized by John the Baptizer! Andrew and I saw you there. John the Baptizer called out when he saw you. He called you the lamb of God. Andrew and I spoke to you afterward. Do you remember?" John had climbed out of the boat and stood face to face with Jesus.

"I remember. That's why I am here speaking to you now," answered Jesus.

"Ho, James, John! How go the nets? Andrew and I follow this new teacher. Will you come as well?" Simon stood by the right shoulder of Jesus and spoke to his fishing partners. Now Andrew drew near and stood beside his brother.

"We will follow you, Master," said John and turned and looked at his brother James. "I must go with them, James. You will come too, won't you?"

Slowly James climbed down out of the boat. He looked at Jesus carefully and then at Simon. "We're brothers, John. If Simon and Andrew can follow this new rabbi, so can we. Lamb of God, you said the one in the wilderness called him." He turned to Jesus. "Sire, if you are the chosen one and you would have us in your company, we will come with you. I ask you to rest with us for a little while. Our father, Zebedee, will return in a short time. We must speak with him before we leave. It is our duty to mend the net so those he must hire to take our place may be equipped for fishing. We are simple fishermen. Will you not tell us of yourself until our father comes?"

"I have walked far this day. I'll gladly rest a while and talk with you." With this Jesus made a place for himself on the shore and the others gathered round to listen while he talked. James, conscientious as always, pulled the net across his knees and went on with the mending while he listened to Jesus. Only Jesus noticed it was Andrew who took the net-mender's tool John had laid aside.

Simon's younger brother sat down beside James and helped him mend the net.

They asked many questions. James began by asking Jesus from where he had come. Where had he spent his early life? Did he know a trade? As Jesus told them of his life in Nazareth and how he had learned the carpenter's trade from Joseph, the others listened so intently they did not hear Zebedee's footsteps until he was upon them.

"Why are you sitting here in idle gossip? The net is still not mended. How can you take out boats with a broken net? John, why is Andrew doing your work? Get back to that net and waste no more time! Simon, Andrew, what are you doing here? It is past time for you to launch your boat. Must I think of everything?" Zebedee was red with anger. His sharp, high-pitched voice cut through the still air.

"The net is nearly mended, Zebedee. I helped James because as you can see, John cut his hand. The work went faster when I helped." Andrew smiled at Zebedee.

"We'll finish mending the net in just a few more minutes, father. We do not go fishing tonight. You'll need to hire men to take our place in the morning. All of us—John, Simon, Andrew, and I— are leaving to follow this new teacher. He is called Jesus of Nazareth." James stood up and faced his angry father. As James stood up, John stood beside him.

For a moment Zebedee could not speak at all. He was so angry he could only wave his arms and stamp his feet. Finally he regained his voice. "What do you mean, you're not taking the boats out tonight? Get this net mended and take the boat out as soon as it's ready! John, go after the other crew members. Get them here quickly! I'll hear no more nonsense about following some teacher from Nazareth."

"James told you rightly, father. We must follow Jesus! You'll find others to take our place in the boats. Try to understand, father. We must go." John's face was as flushed as his father's and his voice trembled as he spoke.

Zebedee turned and looked questioningly at Simon. "Yes, what James said goes for Andrew and me as well. We plan to follow Jesus, Zebedee." Simon answered the question Zebedee had not voiced.

The older man's face had changed from red to purple. He had trouble breathing. At last he regained his calm. He turned and walked away without a word and then turned again and stood facing the group. His voice was calm and hard now.

"You're fools, you know. This is a prosperous business. You could have had everything I've worked to build up. Fishing is all you know. Now who will ever hear your names again? Go ahead, follow this fellow back to Nazareth! You'll have to learn something besides fishing there, if you're to fill your bellies." Zebedee turned and walked away without another word.

There was silence in the group. Stubbornly James sat down and went back to finishing the last bit of mending on the net. John started after his father. He walked a few steps and then turned, came back, and sat beside James.

"Master, will you tell us more about the new way? I thirst to hear more of what you would teach us," said Simon. The quick dark of Palestine fell about them. Jesus pulled his cloak more closely against the chill. Andrew left the group and went off into the darkness. Presently he returned with an armload of driftwood. He placed the wood carefully across some stones and went to the small fire a few yards away where the tar pot used in mending nets rested. With a flat stone Andrew scooped up some coals and placed them beneath the wood. In a moment or two he had blown them into full blaze. The dry wood crackled with the warmth it gave.

The deep, clear voice of Jesus began to speak again. The little group by the fire listened in the still dark.

The Request

In the beginning there were only the four. Then Matthew, a tax collector in Capernaum, was chosen as the fifth. After that came Philip from Bethsaida. Bartholomew, Thomas, James son of Alphaeus, Simon the Zealot, Thaddaeus, and Judas Iscariot followed, and so finally there were twelve. One disciple to represent each of the twelve tribes of Israel. Jesus never said that this was his reason for choosing exactly twelve disciples, but John understood that this must be his reason for selecting twelve men to work with him.

Now came the glorious days when the crowds flocked to hear Jesus speak. At first they were drawn by the gossip of the miracles he had performed—the blind to whom he had given sight, the sick he had restored to health. The word was passed around that even lepers had been healed by Jesus. This was scarcely to be believed. The most famous physicians in all the world had never healed a leper, but this teacher called Jesus was said to have healed lepers with a touch. The crowds came, and when they listened to Jesus they came again. Now they came to hear the words of comfort and joy he spoke. Again and again they came and listened to this new prophet who spoke of a new kind of life. He told them of a new kind of kingdom where there were no oppressors and none who were oppressed. A kingdom where all men were brothers and each cared as much for his fellow as for himself.

John listened with the other disciples, and he believed. John understood Jesus was not speaking of a kingdom he would rule as king on a throne. Nevertheless John's pride made him yearn for a special place among the disciples. One day he took James aside and spoke to him about a plan he had made. "See how the crowds follow our Master, brother. We have seen him make the blind see, even restore life to the widow's son. There is no doubt that Jesus is the Messias. You and I were among the first he called. It is right for us to sit at his right hand and at his left hand when his time has come. If we do not ask, surely some of the others will. Already Simon is the leader of our group. What do you think, James? Shall we ask him for the places of honor at his side?"

"Ask for us both, John. You're better with words than I. I'll go with you. You speak for both of us," said James. So the two brothers went to Jesus. With James at his side John spoke to Jesus.

"Master, we ask that you grant us a favor," began John.

"What is it you want me to do, John?"

"Lord, when you come into your kingdom grant that one of us sit at your right hand and the other at your left hand," said John.

A sadness came over Jesus' face and he turned away. "You don't know what you are saying," he said at last. "Can you drink of the cup I must drink? Can you undergo the suffering I must undergo?"

"Lord, we can," said John, eager to press his claim for favor.

"You will surely drink of my cup and you will suffer as I must suffer, but what you ask is not mine to give." The sad look crossed his face again and Jesus turned and walked away.

John was crestfallen. He had been almost sure Jesus would say yes. His head dropped and he sat down and rested his head in his hands. James patted him on the shoulder and walked away. John stared at the ground. Judas came over to him.

"Why should you ask special favors for your brother and for yourself? What makes you think you should be favored over the rest of us?" he asked.

John was hurt. Already he wished he had not asked Jesus for the special favor. Judas' angry words brought the shame and hurt to the surface in a rush.

"Well, for one thing my brother and I were among the first chosen, and besides I talked with Jesus before he chose anyone!

Since you were *the last one* chosen you haven't much to say about it."

"And because I was chosen last I should have no consideration at all, I suppose," Judas snapped back.

"We must all work together, Judas. I don't believe Jesus thinks of giving preference to any one of us. You heard him tell John he could not grant him what he asked. That settles it. Let's not talk about it anymore," said Andrew, coming up and putting an arm around Judas.

"Well, I suppose there's no use in talking more about it, but John was wrong to expect Jesus to give preference to him and to his brother James." Judas walked away.

"I guess I can't really blame him for being angry, Andrew. I know I was wrong. As soon as the words left my mouth I could see I'd made a mistake. I wonder if I'll ever learn!" John looked more disgusted than ever.

"We've all got plenty to learn. But go a little easier with Judas. As the only Judean among us he's sensitive. He feels a slight more keenly than the rest of us. Simon doesn't like him, and sometimes it shows plainly. I try to help him. I wish you would too," said Andrew. John nodded. He wanted to be alone and to think.

The days passed, and Jesus and his band of twelve traveled in and around Galilee. It seemed somehow that the favor John asked and could not be given brought him closer to Jesus. There was no task John seemed unwilling to do, however menial. Now instead of pressing close to Jesus, as had been his custom before, John seated himself beside Philip and Andrew, who never pushed themselves forward but always stayed in the background. Now it was Jesus who often sought John out and talked with him. Sometimes he would beckon to John to sit beside him while they ate the simple evening meal and would talk to him then. After a while it became customary for John to sit next to Jesus, and it usually was John who walked next to him as they strode the dusty roads of Palestine.

48

Even Peter noticed it and said, pointing to John, "There's the one the Master loves best." Because the big man said it with no trace of jealousy the others smiled and nodded. Only Judas said nothing, and usually it was Judas who sat on the other side of Jesus at the evening meal.

Simon was clearly the leader of the twelve, but it was John who seemed to understand best what Jesus was trying to teach them. Often now it was John to whom the others turned when they did not understand something Jesus had told them. John would sometimes turn to Jesus and say, "Lord, we are simple men. Speak your truth to us more plainly that we may be sure we understand. If we are to help others to know, we must be sure in our own minds."

There were some things John did not wholly understand, but he knew someday it would all be made clear to him. Someday he would have the answer. There were three of the disciples whom Jesus took closer into his confidence than the others. John, Simon who became Simon Peter, and James the brother of John were the three Jesus chose to accompany him on special occasions.

A Village in Samaria

The day was hot and the two travelers were dusty from their long walk. They paused to rest for a moment and gaze at the gray bulk of Mount Gerizim looming up in the distance. A short way ahead a small village spread itself on each side of the road in the shadow of the low mountain. They had come a long way to seek a place where the group might rest together on their way to Jerusalem.

"Seek out a village in Samaria," Jesus had told them. So they had come to ask for lodging.

"We've covered the distance more quickly than I thought, James. Perhaps we can make arrangements for the Master's stay and rejoin the others before darkness comes." It was John, the taller and more slender of the two, who spoke.

"We'll find out soon enough, brother. You know how stubborn these Samaritans are. Instead of being overcome with joy at the opportunity to welcome Jesus and hear him talk, they'll think only of how much they can charge for food and lodging. I hope Judas has money enough in the treasury," responded James. The two brothers walked toward the outskirts of the village. A few yards away they noticed the well in the center of a cluster of houses. This was always the best place to get information, so they turned off the road to speak to the group of women at the well.

"Where can we find the elder of the village?" inquired John. For a few seconds the women just stared at the two strangers. At last one young girl pointed to a house on the opposite side of the road. The taller brother smiled and nodded his thanks. Quickly both men crossed the road to the house. James raised his hand to knock on the door but the door opened before he could knock. A man, very old and small of stature, stepped through the door. He frowned as he looked at his two visitors.

"You'll be strangers to this village, I think," he said.

"Strangers we are, and come to bring you the good news that our Master, the Lord Jesus, will stop at this very village. We seek lodging for him and for the twelve disciples in his company. My brother James and I are to make arrangements. I am John."

"I am Michri, chief of this village. Make your arrangements somewhere else. There is no place in this village to care for your Master whoever he may be. You Jews set your faces toward Jerusalem. We are Samaritans. Our holy place is yonder on Mount Gerizim. Our Mount Gerizim was old when Jerusalem was no more than a place for sheep to graze." The old man began to laugh in a high-pitched cackle. Before the astonished brothers could say a word, he turned on his heel and went back into the house, slamming the door shut after him.

John was the first to recover his speech. His face red with anger, he pounded on the closed door and shouted, "Open the door! I command you in the name of our Lord Jesus, open the door! You'll regret this insult." John was out of breath with all his pounding and shouting. Now James began to shout.

"Michri, if that's what you call yourself, come out here. Can't you understand what we're saying? It's Jesus, the Messias, for whom we have come to arrange lodging."

Once more the door opened. This time a tall young man stood in the door. "You've heard all my father has to say to you. Either leave at once or I'll call my brothers. We'll throw you both out of this village. Leave and don't come back, and don't bring your Jesus fellow here either." The young man was not smiling and his right hand grasped a heavy wooden staff. He stood in the doorway and looked straight at John and James.

"Come, James, we'll report back to the Master. He'll make short work of these scoundrels." John beckoned to his brother and the two of them left the house and turned back toward the road. The young man in the doorway watched them.

"You've not seen the last of us," shouted James as they started back down the road they had come. The two travelers walked more slowly on their trip back to rejoin Jesus and the other disciples. There was little talk between them. The anger boiled inside each brother. John began to think about the lesson Jesus would teach these rude, arrogant Samaritans. He smiled to himself. It would do his heart good to see that old man and his stubborn son humbled. Already he could hear them apologizing for their rudeness and begging forgiveness. He turned to his brother.

"Come, James. Let's hurry. I'm anxious to report this matter to

51

Jesus." The two brothers redoubled their speed. In another hour they recrossed the border back into Galilee. Not much later they came in sight of an open field from which people were moving away in different directions. As they came nearer, the two disciples could see Jesus still talking to a few of those standing near him. Behind him in a small group talking among themselves sat the other ten disciples.

When John and James approached, Jesus smiled and beckoned them to come closer. They stood by his side, waiting as he spoke to those who lingered. At last Jesus was free and turned to them.

"Did you find a place for us to stay? What greetings do you bring from our Samaritan brothers across the border?"

"Brothers! You won't call them brothers when you hear how they received us!" John was so indignant the words fairly burst from him.

"They told us there was no place for us in their village. The chief of the village and his son threatened to throw us out of the village," James took up the story.

"Shall we call down fire from heaven to consume these men who do not receive us?" asked John.

"John, John, don't you know I've come to save men's lives, not to destroy them? I think I named you two correctly when I called you Sons of Thunder. You're just as fiery as your father." Jesus smiled again, but he shook his head sadly at the two hot-tempered disciples. "We'll go to Jerusalem by another way. Do you remember when I first spoke to you while you mended nets? I told you the way would not be easy. Not everyone will believe in what we do, in what we teach. We must have the patience to make them believe without destroying them."

"Go by another way? Master, they'll call us cowards. What kind of men can we be if we will not fight for you!" John almost shouted the words.

"Go sit down and think on what I have just said." Jesus spoke the words almost sternly. "Come back to me when you have truly considered what I am saying to you."

John walked away to sit by himself. Gradually his temper cooled. Sometime later he went back to Jesus and stood before him.

"Master, from now on, no matter what happens I will not lose my temper. You have taught me a second lesson today. I will not let my temper get away again."

"A second lesson, John?"

"Yes, Lord. You remember when James and I asked you for the privilege of sitting someday at your right hand and your left hand. You told us then we would suffer the hard things you must suffer but you could not grant us any special place. I understood then. We must be content to do our work and serve you in any way we can. I haven't forgotten that lesson and I won't forget to hold my temper. It won't be easy. I've always been hot-headed."

"Sons of Thunder I called you and James. Now I think you're learning to be gentle, John. It takes a certain kind of courage not to be afraid of loving people. Even people who may not understand what love really is. I think that's something you're beginning to learn. We must learn to love each other. It's very hard to do sometimes, but it's the only way. Learn to love people, John—all people."

Golgotha

The sky was very dark. It was an early dark before the hour of nightfall. It was not the soft darkness of night. The sky hung low.

Dark, rolling clouds boiled angrily, and yet there was no breath of wind. The air was heavy and still. No sound of birds was heard. No birds flew hunting a place of refuge. This was strange. Usually in the last minutes before a storm broke birds could be heard and seen darting frantically across the sky in search of some safe place. The heavy clouds tossing in the sky came lower and lower.

The tall, spare young man stood there with the four women beside him. He stood on the top of the low hill and gazed with clear eyes at the cross above him. There was great sadness in his look, and his eyes were filled with sorrow but they did not turn away. The women beside him stood erect, hands clasped before them, gazing at the cross. They looked steadily upward without flinching. The earlier tears had dried on their cheeks. All of the sorrow and agony of waiting had been wrung from them. Now only their love for the one on the cross remained.

The tall man looked at the cross before him and widened his gaze to include the two other crosses on either side. He gasped slightly. "That is what he meant," he thought to himself, and he remembered Jesus' words, "Can you drink of the cup I must drink?"

The tall man's own words came back to mock him—"Grant that one of us sit at your right hand and one at your left hand." Hot tears of shame rushed to his eyes. He knelt beside the four women and buried his face in the folds of his cloak and prayed a silent prayer. "Master, forgive again my arrogance and pride. I asked to share your glory when I should have asked to share your burden. Lord, grant me forgiveness now and, if there be years ahead for me, let me also earn a cross. Only now when I begin to understand completely you leave me. Lord, there is so much for me to learn." He could add no more to his small prayer. He stood, and moving his arm slightly drew the woman next to him a little closer.

Her head came only to his shoulder, for he was well above medium height. The woman was weary, but the arm about her shoulder seemed to comfort her. She turned her head slightly and the hint of a sad smile flickered on her face. The group had been standing, sometimes kneeling, for several hours. The tall man's name was John. He was John, son of Zebedee. Next to him stood Mary, mother of Jesus; beyond her, Mary Magdalene; next Salome, John's own mother; and then Mary, wife of Cleopas, mother of James-the-Less.

Only a few minutes before, John had heard the voice of him he loved most speak to them. John knew no matter what lay ahead he could never forget those words. Of all the disciples he alone was there to hear them. The words would be a part of his life for as long as he lived.

"Woman, behold thy son," Jesus had said to Mary. She had been looking up at Jesus as he spoke. She caught the meaning of his words and instantly turned her eyes to John. "Behold thy mother," Jesus spoke again, directing his words to John. John moved closer to Mary and put his arm around her. John could not answer. His heart was too full. Instead he knelt and spoke his silent prayer.

From that instant on he would give Mary all the care and devotion a son could give a mother. Jesus looked down on them and was content. Until this moment he had fought off the pain and weariness. A moment later the final words came: "It is finished."

As she heard the last words, Mary clutched her throat and turned to John. John drew her closer to him. He heard the words and understood their meaning. "It is finished" meant this pain, this sacrifice, is done with. All that Jesus had taught his disciples, all that he had shared with them, was still there. Those truths would never be finished! John was not sure how he and the other disciples would find a way to take the message of Jesus to the people everywhere, but he knew they must find a way.

Joseph of Arimathea had taken his courage in his hands and gone to Pilate and requested to be allowed to bury Jesus in his own tomb. Since Joseph was a man of influence and wealth, Pilate granted his request. Now Joseph approached the group. John welcomed him as a friend and follower of Jesus. Gratefully Mary and John listened to his request to prepare the body of Jesus for burial in his own tomb.

Soon after Joseph came Nicodemus, another friend, bearing the linen cloths and ointments for burial. Seeing that Mary was so weary and overcome by grief, Joseph urged John to take her to their lodging place to rest. At last Mary was persuaded. John with Mary and Salome turned down the hill toward the city, leaving the other two women with Joseph and Nicodemus.

Slowly they walked through the streets of Jerusalem. Was this the same Jerusalem often called the "Golden City"? It had no look of gold now. There was no sun to turn the limestone buildings to the color of gold. The crowds usually found in the streets were gone. The few people who were about scurried in one direction or another. All seemed eager to get home. It was if everyone wanted to be off the streets. There was a strange silence in the city. Only the thud of wooden shutters being closed broke the silence. Shopkeepers hurried to close their shops. It was earlier than the usual hour of closing. The ever-present camels, donkey carts, and men on horseback clogging the narrow streets were not in sight now. The members of the Sanhedrin and their followers who had been so insistent on putting Jesus to death no longer shouted in the streets.

In the distance a file of Roman soldiers clanked their armored way toward a guard post somewhere in the city. The clouds which from early morning on had hung low and angry over Jerusalem began to lift slightly and move slowly north. John felt the first stirring of a breeze upon his cheek. He looked up and watched the dark clouds move more swiftly in the sky, away from Jerusalem. They moved north toward Galilee. Were the clouds dark messengers taking the sad news to Nazareth that the carpenter's son was dead?

John had only a moment to let his fancy linger. The wind rose higher, though blowing gently still, pushing the dark mass of clouds free of the city and sending them racing north. There was an instant of half light, and then the sudden night of Palestine descended. The darkness was softer now. The breeze turned warmer. Just as they reached the doorway of the house John and the two women turned again to look at the sky. Wherever they looked they could see the stars appear.

The house was very quiet. Mary and Salome slept. In a small room off the much larger room on the upper floor John lay on a narrow bed. He was tired, but there was so much to remember sleep would not come. He lay on his back, arms folded beneath his head, and gazed through the tiny window of the room. He could see only the smallest bit of black sky. He thought of the days just past.

More than most of the other disciples—perhaps more than *any* of the other disciples—John had paid attention to the warnings Jesus had given them as they journeyed to Jerusalem. There had been that day at Lazarus' house in Bethany. Mary, the sister of Lazarus, had brought out a costly ointment made of spikenard to anoint Jesus. She showed her gratitude because he had brought Lazarus back to life. Judas suggested selling the ointment to raise money for the poor, but Jesus said, "She has kept this against the day of my burying." The words brought a chill to John. He owed Jesus so much! He had come to Jesus an arrogant, hot-tempered man full of pride. For years he had quarreled bitterly with his father. Life with Jesus had changed that.

The temper was still there, but he had learned to control it. Arrogance had been replaced by the realization that serving others could be more rewarding than seeking a place of honor. Building the cooking fires, helping to prepare the evening meals, walking the dusty roads of Galilee helped keep any man's pride in place. John the disciple was not the same John who had flung down his net-mender's tool in a fit of anger so many months before.

And then what Jesus had told them would happen *had* happened. They had come to Jerusalem to celebrate the Passover. With Simon Peter, John had made the arrangements for the Passover supper. The scenes flashed through John's mind again. The last supper, the walk to the Garden of Gethsemane, the waiting there. Then Judas had come with the soldiers! Jesus had been led away. John had followed and had been with Jesus as he stood before Caiaphas and Annas. He had been nearby when Pilate had turned Jesus over to the Sanhedrin and allowed him to be sentenced to death.

John had gone to Mary, waiting in her room. When she knew the news she insisted on going to Golgotha. Jesus was her son. She would go to him! She would stand there as near to him as she could be. She would share those last hours in the only way she could. Mary Magdalene, Salome, and Mary, wife of Cleopas, accompanied her. John led the way.

The memory of the past hours was almost more than John could bear. What could they do now? Tomorrow he would have to find James and Simon Peter. They would have to gather the others together. Somehow they must plan together how to carry on.

Love One Another

He was very old. A bishop of the church who had labored for long in many lands, now confined to his chair and carried daily to the church through the school to greet the children. That was all that was left to him. He was so old his memory played tricks on him. Only a few days ago he had decided to write a letter to his brother James. He had dictated for some minutes to his writing clerk when he suddenly remembered—his brother had been dead for more years than he could remember.

Wearily he had shaken his head, dismissed the startled clerk, and asked to be alone. He knew his time was not far off. He welcomed death. Once more he would be reunited with Jesus and the others. Of all the twelve he was the last. There was one regret. If only he could have merited a glorious death like the others. His brother James had been the first to go—felled by Herod's sword in Jerusalem. Though they had been but twelve—and Paul, of course —they had kept the faith, and the word had spread throughout the world.

Now he alone of that small band was left. There would be no glorious death on the cross for him, no swift blow from an executioner's sword. Only the quiet running out of time for an old man who had tried to understand and teach his understanding to others. He frowned and rapped his cane against the wooden leg of his chair. And then he smiled. He was past ninety and still the flicker of the old temper remained. There was still a trace of pride he could not subdue.

Hearing the noise of the cane against the chair, the old man's servant hurried quickly to his side. "Sire, is something wrong?"

"Rouse me early in the morning and take me to the church. It will be for the last time. Early, mind you. Very early. There is not much time left." The old man waved his servant away. He wanted to be alone with his memories.

He tried to make his mind reach back to the early days in Galilee. The distance was too great. He could not make his mind recall. The one thing he remembered best were the words Jesus had taught him long ago: "Love all people, John—all people." He had tried to practice that teaching all his life since Jesus had changed him and his life. The people often smiled affectionately

59

when he was carried into the church. He would lean down from his chair and touch their heads and say, "Love one another, children, love one another." The people would nod their heads and smile.

Once someone has asked him why he stressed this charge above all others. Smiling to himself now, he recalled his answer. "Love one another. It is enough to remember this. If you do this all the other commandments follow. This is the hardest of them all. Love one another."

Suddenly he was so tired, so tired. He seemed to see a blaze of bright light—a light like he had seen once long ago on Mount Hermon. The cane dropped from his hand. Tomorrow was already here for John.

JAMES
Man of Action

TO:

My Beloved Brother John, Disciple of our Lord Jesus

I give you greetings and hope that the bearer of this letter finds you in good health and happy in the work of the church. This will be the last communication between us, for my time is near at hand. Tomorrow, or the day after, or the day beyond that, I will surely die. Herod Agrippa, the king, seeks favor with the Sanhedrin. Josias, one of the chief among them, clamors for my blood.

He has said to Herod, "It is James who leads the Nazarenes, that group of strange fanatics who flout our priests and sacred law. James claims that Jesus whom we crucified rose from the dead and appeared among the members of his company on numerous occasions. Such claims make James a blasphemer and liable for punishment by death." Herod readily agreed. There is discontent in Rome with Herod's rule in Judea. The king is anxious to have no more hint of local trouble reach the Emperor's ears.

So I am in prison. I die when Herod chooses to strike the blow. It cannot be long. That I can write this letter is through the kindness of my jailor who, though not one of us, has sympathy for our teachings. The young lad who will seek to find you with this letter is called Chilion. I commend him to your care and teaching. He has learned some from me, but you will teach him much more.

My thoughts turn back now to the real beginning of our new life. No, I do not turn my thoughts to Galilee, though that too was a beginning. I think now of that most glorious day which followed after our time of greatest dread and sorrow. As I write I pause more often than I should, for time flies so quickly by. I pause and gaze at the wall before me. There is no window in my cell. And through the dark stone of the wall my eyes see back to yesterday, and I can hear your voice.

"James, James! What good fortune I have found you! He has risen! Jesus is not in the tomb. We were there. Peter and I both were there! I tell you our Master has risen from the dead!" Oh, how your voice rang with the good news and how my own heart beat faster as I heard your words! Then I went with you and with Peter, searching for the others. At last we found them all, except for Andrew and Thomas. We went to the room where we had eaten Passover, and soon Andrew came to join us, but Thomas still was not among us. So we were but ten. Judas, who betrayed our Lord, had gone from us. Even now I cannot bring myself to write the words that tell his shame. Ah, the desolation and grief we shared, brother. Our despair was deep. Remembering heightens the memory of our joy when in those next few moments that little room was filled with the glory of our Lord's presence. Suddenly *he* was there and we were not alone. He talked with us, and it was then we knew somehow we could do the tasks he set us to do. He left us but appeared again, and this time Thomas was among us, and Thomas' disbelief that we had actually talked with Jesus and seen him was taken from him as he saw our Lord and spoke with him.

And there were other times we saw Jesus before he took his final leave of us. As we fished that evening, where we had cast our nets so many earlier times—before we knew our Lord—you saw Jesus on the shore and recognized him first before the rest of us. But that was not strange. He loved you so. He loved us all, including Judas, who betrayed him, but he had a special kind of love for you, my brother. So we went about our work, and it fell to me to speak for the church in Jerusalem. I was glad to have you by my side as you worked with me and cared for Mary. Those were hard days, but we had so much life in us no task could be too hard for us. We were men born again. I say that was our new beginning—starting from the time when you came running to me with the news that Jesus had risen from the tomb.

These later years which took you away from Jerusalem to spread the word to such cities as Babylon, Smyrna, and Ephesus have kept us far apart. I wish I could see you once again, but that I know cannot be. I have done the work here as best I could and, though there are many who fight against our teachings, still the people listen. Our numbers are few but they grow each day. May you live to see the time when people throughout many lands will learn of Jesus and his teachings and follow him. Surely if such a rough fisherman as I can learn to follow him, and face death unafraid, for truly I have no fear in me of this death that I must face, others will come also.

What more is there for me to say? I wish that we could have found a way to bring our father into our fellowship before his death. I fear he died before we found a way to make our peace between us and him. I have always sorrowed about that. I am glad our mother, Salome, believed as we believed and helped us in our work as best she could. Soon I will see her again. So, my brother and fellow disciple, I close this letter. Chilion will wait to leave until my death is sure so that he may tell you of the end. Again I commend the lad to your care and teaching. He is strong in the faith and can be another arm for you to use. The church here will continue on. There are those who will not let the teachings die. My death is only Herod's gesture to the Sanhedrin. A bow toward Rome to show them he is the master here. You and I know there is only one Master, and his name is Jesus. I go soon to join him. Work for the kingdom of our Lord and keep strong in the faith.

Your brother and fellow disciple, James.

Chilion's Story

He was no more than twenty. A young man with the dark hair and eyes common to his race. He had traveled a long, long way—from Jerusalem to Ephesus. He waited, and in a short while the tall man came toward him.

"I am John. You seek me?"

"Sire, my name is Chilion. I come from Jerusalem. I bring a letter from your brother James."

"A letter to me, from James? It's been so long since I have heard from him. Tell me, how do things go with him in Jerusalem?" John held his hand out for the parchment the youth had taken from his pouch.

"Perhaps you'd best read the letter first and then I will tell you all I know." Chilion handed over the parchment to John.

John nodded his head and motioned the young man to sit beside him as he read. Chilion watched the expression on John's face as he read and saw the pain. The tall man's face turned sad, and then a deeper sadness came into his eyes. But as he read more, he smiled. Then his expression became sad again. Finally he put down the parchment and turned to Chilion with the question for which the young man waited.

"How did my brother die?" John asked.

"He died so bravely I cannot tell it well enough, but I will do my best. . ."

Your brother gave me the letter he had written you and asked me to wait until after his death to leave so that I might bring you news of how he died.

He had been accused by Josias, a member of the Sanhedrin. Josias had gone to Herod Agrippa many times to complain of the teachings of James and of our people. We seemed to be a particular annoyance to Caiaphas, and he used Josias to pour accusations against us into Herod's ear. There were rumors that Rome was not pleased with Herod's rule. By striking a blow at our church he would seem to set an example of firmness and placate the Sanhedrin as well. Thus he would please both Rome and Caiaphas.

Herod ordered James to be imprisoned, but this was not enough for Caiaphas. He had Josias complain to Herod that since James was a blasphemer for saying that Jesus had risen from the dead, James deserved to be put to death. This Herod finally consented to do, but he would not crucify James. He feared another crucifixion would so arouse the followers of James that another disturbance would be created.

The third day after James was imprisoned, Herod sent for him to be brought before him. "Have you anything to say for yourself?" asked Herod. "Know you any reason why one blasphemer should not die like another?"

Your brother James was not a tall man, as you know. Though broad of shoulder he stood shorter than myself. Yet somehow it seemed he grew taller than any of us there who watched him as he stood before the king. "I know no reason why I merit better treatment than my Lord and Master, Jesus Christ, who died not because of the charges brought against him by these hypocrites. My Master died on the cross to prove the truth of what he taught. Jesus died, but he rose from the dead and now lives in his own kingdom to die no more.

"You may kill me, for I am only a man subject to death as any man. You will not kill the teachings of our Lord, nor will you keep the people from following what they know is truth. Josias has been the messenger of Caiaphas, coaxing you to put me to death because I am the leader of our people here who follow Jesus of Nazareth. Josias thinks, get rid of James and these Nazarenes will soon disperse and forget what he has taught them. He is wrong. In Judea, Samaria, Galilee, and all the other lands the good news of Jesus speaks to all the people through the mouths of those of us he chose.

"Dispose of James as you must and will. You only put to death a man. You cannot kill the word of God. Now do with me what you must. I have no more to say."

Your brother stood there straight and unafraid. Herod's face was flushed, and anger and fear were written in the look he turned on James. Before he could say a word Josias, who had been standing behind the king, came forward to kneel by James. "I am the one who persecuted you," he said. "And yet your words have turned my heart. Better to die with such faith as yours than live with the old lies of Caiaphas. I beg your forgiveness. I stand with you. If I die with you, can you take me to your Christ?"

"Forgiven you are, and willingly," said James, raising up Josias beside him. "Our Lord Jesus died for us all. Those who will believe in him must surely see him when he is ready to receive them."

Now Herod Agrippa rose to his feet and roared at his soldiers standing by. "Hand me your sword," he commanded the nearest one. "I'll speed the way for these fools who court death so lovingly."

Herod took the sword in both his hands and swung it. Josias was beheaded where he stood. Herod swung the sword again and James was dead.

That is the way your brother died, and I have reported to you all I know. Each word that was said I committed to my memory that you might have a faithful account of how it happened. Your brother was a man of courage. Because my father was the jailor where your brother was imprisoned I came to know him well. Almost every day I brought him food and he talked with me. He told me of his early life and of the one called Jesus who died but somehow lives. I did not understand, but I could follow such a man as your brother. He told me you could make me understand what he had little time to tell. And so I brought his letter to you.

John stood up. There were tears in his eyes. He placed his hand on Chilion's shoulder. "I must be alone to think and pray for a little time," he said. "I will see that food and a place to rest are provided for you. Later we will talk. James commended you to my teaching and care. I do not know whether there is more that I can teach you or not. It seems to me my brother has already taught you more than most of us know. Perhaps there are things we can teach each other. Come, Chilion, I'll see you to your resting place and then we'll talk again." Holding the last words of James in his hand, John with Chilion walked from the room.

PHILIP
Who Was Content to Follow

"Master, when you consider others for your company I ask you to think of Philip. He is a good man—as good as any of us. He heard you preach in the synagogue and twice he has been in the crowds who listened as you talked since then. I know him well. So do Andrew, James, and John." For almost a week Simon had been thinking about those he felt should be considered by Jesus. Ever since Jesus had indicated he would need others to work with him in this special way, Simon had considered first one person and then another. At last he decided Philip was the person he could recommend most highly.

Jesus' grave smile was Simon's answer. After a while Jesus

left the others where they were resting on a low hill on the outskirts of Capernaum. Jesus left them and went into the city.

The sailmaker's shop was one long, low room. The sailmaker and his assistant were on their knees pushing their heavy needles through the cloth. The assistant was a man of thirty and strongly built. Though his occupation kept him largely indoors, too many Galilean suns had bronzed his skin to permit it to become as pale as his employer's. The man who stood in the doorway judged the younger man had not always sewed sails for a livelihood.

"Is it a sail you require?" Tahath, the sailmaker, was on his feet, leaving the younger man to finish the seam.

"No, I would speak with Philip," replied the man in the doorway.

"My helper is too busy to talk now. See him after the shop is closed. We've only time for work now, if you have no business here." Tahath turned back to his work.

"Follow me," the stranger said, and looked Philip full in the face. The sailmaker's helper returned his look, crouching over the sail on which he was working.

Philip looked over at Tahath and then back at Jesus standing in the doorway. Slowly he put down the long needle he was using. He stood up. Only now was it possible to notice his left arm, which was drawn stiffly into his waist and bent at the elbow. Philip stepped on the cloth in his bare feet, picked up his sandals just inside the door, and followed Jesus to the street. He paused for a moment and thrust his feet into his sandals, pulled the straps tight, and hurried after Jesus, who was three steps ahead of him.

Hurrying, Philip caught up with Jesus. "Teacher, can we not talk here? If I am away from the shop for long, Tahath will turn me out. He's not one to permit conversation to take the place of business."

Jesus stopped and faced Philip. "What need is there of talk, Philip? I have seen you in the crowds that gathered while I spoke to them. You listened, and by your eyes I could see you heard and believed. I need you in my company."

"Me?" Philip asked. "I saw Simon, James, Andrew, John, and Matthew gathered near you as you spoke. It is said they follow you. What can I add when you have such as they? As you can see," he pointed to his left arm, "there are not many tasks a man can do with just one arm."

"You can do the tasks I have for you. You will be an arm of God in your new work just as the others are. It was Simon who asked me to consider you when I chose others to complete our company of twelve. Even had he not spoken, I would have sought you out." Jesus turned and began walking. Philip walked beside him.

"Lord, if you have chosen me, then surely I will follow. I am not like the others. Simon and James were always our leaders as boys and when we fished together. Andrew speaks more slowly than his brother, but his words are listened to. John is the thinker among us, though his hot temper brings him sometimes into trouble despite his head for understanding. Matthew I do not know well, for there was little we had to pass through the tax collector's booth. Men say that he is just. But Master, I am a plain man, poor, as you can see. My mother, who was Greek, taught me her language and something of her people's history. From the good *hazzan* who taught us in our school I learned like my fellows. My father fished as all men in Bethsaida do. So I too fished—but that was before this." Philip moved his left arm slightly.

"And what of your arm, Philip? How did you injure it?"

"We were members of one of the crews of Zebedee. One night the wind, which comes up from the west suddenly as a snake strikes without warning, caught us too near the eastern wall of rock which rises sheer above the sea. Our crew fought the wind like men possessed. We had almost won free when a giant wave slammed against our boat. My father was washed overboard and

70

my arm was smashed. Shortly after that the wind died down and we made it back to shore. When my arm healed I could no longer fish. Tahath took me on as his assistant. And so you found me there."

Their walk had brought them through the city. Now they approached the place where the other disciples waited. "Go speak with the others," Jesus said. Jesus himself drew apart to be alone and to pray and meditate.

His old friends greeted Philip warmly, for they had all been boys together in Bethsaida. Then Matthew came up to the new disciple.

"Welcome, Philip. Welcome to our company. I was a publican, you know, until our Master let me become one of these few who work with him. A tax collector makes few friends, so more than the others I value this opportunity for new friends. I would be your friend and have you for mine."

"I have always heard men speak of you as a just publican, Matthew. Since we are followers of Jesus we are already friends, but I think we could have been friends in any case. Thank you for your greeting."

The days were hard for Philip. He listened carefully to all that Jesus said both to his disciples when they gathered around him to hear his teachings and when he talked to the crowds. Still, even though he listened carefully, Philip did not always understand. Once Jesus said, "Do not give too much thought to what you will eat or what you will drink, nor even the clothes you will wear. There is more to life than meat, and the body is more important than the clothes we put on it. Look at the birds of the air. They neither sow nor reap. They don't gather crops into barns, and yet they are fed by our Heavenly Father. Aren't you much more important to him than the birds?"

All his life Philip had been taught that it was necessary to worry constantly about how to put food on the table, how to find clothes to wear. His father had been a poor man. They had never actually gone hungry, but most times there had been just enough and no more. His Greek mother had told both Philip and his sister, Mariamne, wonderful stories of her country about kings and queens, princesses and princes. But the stories were only dreams his mother spun to amuse her children and to take her own mind away from the hard life they lived.

Years before his father was drowned in the storm on the Sea of Galilee, Philip's mother had died. Philip had done what a boy of twelve could do to help his father and to look after his younger sister. At fifteen he had taken a place in the boats. When he was twenty-two his father was drowned and Philip suffered a crippled arm. Things had been very hard for Philip and Mariamne then. Had it not been for the help of his friends and neighbors they would have been in desperate circumstances. All his life Philip had been practical, methodical, and careful. Not to worry about where the next meal was coming from was contrary to everything he had been taught and everything he had lived. He knew Jesus was saying something which his ears could not hear. It worried Philip. He had not hesitated when Jesus called him, and he would never waver, but how could he understand?

The disciples had accompanied Jesus to a wedding at Cana. Jesus attended because the bridegroom was a friend of his family. He wished to honor an old friend and brought his disciples with him. Now they rested a while after the bridal procession before returning to the bridal feast.

"John, I'm troubled about what Jesus said a few days ago. I've thought and thought and still I do not understand." Philip spoke to John.

"What words of the Master trouble you, Philip?" asked John.

"You recall when he said we were not to give too much thought to what we ate or drank or the clothes we need? He pointed out that birds didn't sow crops or store up any food and yet they were provided for. If God looks after birds, he'll look after us. But it never was that way with our family. We always had to work hard for whatever we had. Why, after the storm when I was hurt and my father was drowned, we would have starved if it hadn't been for our neighbors and friends. Believe me, I was worried then! I know Jesus is trying to point out something, but I don't understand it. Can you explain it?" asked Philip.

"In a way I think you've answered your own question, Philip," said John. "I think Jesus is trying to tell us that God loves us all and looks after us all. I think he means that God expects us to do all we can to try and help ourselves, but that we shouldn't think *only* of what we need to eat and drink and what we need to wear. God will somehow provide for us just as he provides for all his creatures. You know when your father was drowned and you were hurt and could not work for a time, things looked pretty bad for you and Mariamne. But there were people who cared and who helped out. Don't you think God had something to do with that?"

"Of course, of course—now I understand! You must think I am the most dull-witted person our Master could have chosen! And so I am! Your mother, Salome, was the first person to come to our house. She brought food and helped Mariamne nurse me until I was well again. And Bartholomew came every day. It was Bartholomew who helped me find a place with Tahath. What a friend Bartholomew has always been. Your mother's belief in God made her want to help me! Bartholomew believes in God so he helped me when I couldn't do anything for myself! That's it, isn't it?" Philip's voice had risen higher. There was a look of such blazing happiness on his face it made him look like a different person.

"I told you I thought you'd answered your own question, Philip.

73

You're no more dull-witted than the rest of us. We've been with Jesus longer than you. We're beginning to learn what he means. Sometimes it's like trying to reason out a riddle for all of us. Come on, let's join the others," answered John.

"You go on, John. I've just thought of how I can pay an old debt and at the same time contribute to our Master's cause. I wondered why he chose me. Now I think I can do something that will justify his faith in me! I'll not be gone long." Philip smiled at John. The look of happiness still making his face glow, he hurried down the road to Cana. John shook his head wonderingly. He'd never seen careful, methodical Philip so excited before.

"Bartholomew, I've found him! Come with me, I have found the Messias! I've found him, the chosen one of Israel!" Philip stood in front of the small cottage and shouted. In a moment a man about his own age emerged, not from the house but from under the widespread boughs of the fig tree which stood just to the right of the door.

"Were I deaf as my old grandfather I could have heard you a mile away. What's all the shouting about, my friend? I've never known you to be so excited before, Philip." It was Bartholomew who had come out from under the fig tree.

"Bartholomew, I have found the Messias. Jesus of Nazareth! You must come with me to meet and speak with him!" Philip was still breathing hard. He had run much of the way to the village.

"Nazareth? What good can come out of Nazareth?" laughed Bartholomew. "You know I am from Cana. Cana and Nazareth are old rivals."

"This is nothing to make jokes about, Bartholomew. I mean it. Jesus of Nazareth is truly the Messias. Once you talk with him you will know as I know. I've seen him do wonderful things. You know how we studied the scriptures together. Remember, when you came each day while my arm was healing? You took my place in the boat and helped Mariamne look after me. And when

74

you weren't fishing we studied the scriptures together. Once you've talked with Jesus you'll know as I do. He really is the Messias. I am one of his followers and I want to bring you to him. Will you come?"

"I think I must go with you, Philip. We've been good friends for a long time, but I've never known you to be so positive before. I'll go with you. Come, show me the way to your Master." Bartholomew walked away from the small house with his arm around Philip.

Philip and Bartholomew walked up to where Jesus was sitting.

"Master, this is my friend Bartholomew. I have brought him to you. He is my best friend," said Philip.

"Behold an Israelite in whom there is no guile." Jesus spoke directly to Bartholomew.

"Sir, many Israelites are honest men and take no unfair advantage of any man."

"Truly spoken, Bartholomew. I meant only to pay tribute to your own forthrightness," said Jesus.

"How do you know me?" asked Bartholomew.

"I saw you before Philip brought you here," answered Jesus. "I saw you in your private place under the fig tree."

"Philip talked to me on our way here. He told me of the many wonderful things he had seen you do. He told me a little of your teachings. You teach that God loves us all and makes no distinction between men. Lord, I see what Philip has told me is true. You *are* the Messias. I ask leave to serve with you and be your follower. May I march in your company?" asked Bartholomew.

"Come and be one of us, Bartholomew. As you are Philip's true friend, so shall you be mine—and friend to all of us," Jesus answered.

Philip was overjoyed and presented Bartholomew to the others. Six disciples had journeyed from Capernaum to Cana. Now there were seven. Philip was happier than he could ever remember. He had persuaded Bartholomew to come and talk with Jesus, and Jesus had chosen Bartholomew to be one of them. No matter how little else I am able to do, thought Philip, I brought Bartholomew to our Master. That is the best contribution I could have made! In helping Bartholomew get to know Jesus I am beginning to repay him for all his help to me.

Others came and were chosen as the days passed, and at last there were twelve. Philip was never to be bold and assertive. Many times he puzzled long hours trying to understand the meaning of some of the parables Jesus used in his teachings. But Philip always persisted, and his faith in Jesus never wavered.

Jesus called his disciples together and said to them, "I want you to go out in pairs. Spread out to all the villages and teach the people what I have been teaching you about the love of God for all people. When you are ready, come back to me at this place."

Bartholomew and Philip went together. This was a difficult task for Philip. He had worked hard to learn all that Jesus had taught them, but he was not a leader. Nevertheless Jesus had told them to go out and preach to the people, and Philip would do his best. When they came to the first village Bartholomew spoke to the people in the village. Philip went out to those who worked in the fields.

Out into the wheatfields went Philip, where he found a group of men cultivating the wheat. It was a hot task and they were glad of a chance to stop and listen to a stranger speak to them. Philip began telling them of Jesus of Nazareth, the Messias who had come as the chosen one of Israel to restore the kingdom. He told them of what Jesus had said about God's love for all men. He told them how Jesus had restored the sight to blind men and healed sick people. "Even lepers he has made clean and healed. This with my own eyes I have seen," Philip told them.

Some of the men had heard of Jesus, for by now his name was being passed from mouth to mouth through much of Galilee. "You have really seen this Jesus of Nazareth make sick people well? You have seen him make blind men see?" asked one man.

"This I have seen with my own eyes," answered Philip.

"Ah, well, if that is so why doesn't he make your crooked arm well? I see you hold it stiffly and that it does not hang free as it should. What about that? Can't your Master make you well?" As the man spoke to Philip, others in the group nodded their heads questioningly.

"Jesus can make my arm perfect in a moment if he chooses to do so. Once I asked him to make my arm well because I feared I could not do the work he required of me with only one good arm. He told me that he had chosen me as I am with my lame arm. 'I will never ask you to carry a burden too heavy for your shoulders, Philip,' he told me. 'Your lame left arm is only a physical handicap. You'll overcome it without my healing it.' And that is so. Before, when I had to quit fishing and become a sailmaker's apprentice, I was always conscious of my stiff arm. It worried me, and I was always afraid if I did not do my work quickly enough Tahath would dismiss me. Now I never think of my arm. It does for me whatever needs to be done. Let me show you."

Quickly Philip took a hoe and finished cultivating the row where the man who questioned him had been loosening the earth around the young wheat. He went to the next row, and using both hands he pulled the weeds away from the wheat. It was true the stiff arm bent out at an angle different from the good arm, but the weeds were pulled just as well as if he had had two perfect arms.

"Your Master must be powerful for you to have such faith in him. You wear your stiff arm proudly like the Roman soldiers wear the plumes on their helmets. When your Master comes this way we will go to hear him. Bring him to us when it is time for the harvest. We grow good wheat here. We'll bake him bread

77

he won't forget." It was the man who had questioned Philip speaking again and smiling. The man placed his hands on both of Philip's shoulders and bade him farewell.

Philip had been nervous and a little afraid when he first went out to speak to the people in the fields. Now he felt happier than he had ever been. Perhaps he was learning to be a disciple. He turned back toward the village to find Bartholomew. He found him in the center of the village surrounded by many of the villagers.

Bartholomew was almost through speaking. He used some of the parables Jesus had used and explained them so clearly that some in the crowd laughed and others cheered. When Bartholomew finished speaking, the villagers pressed in on him and kept asking him more about Jesus. At last it was time for them to go. Philip shook his head. "I don't see how you do it, Bartholomew. I talked with four men working in a wheatfield and I was nervous and afraid. I kept on because I knew Jesus had sent us to do this work, but I could never have made a speech like you did. There must have been more than thirty people pressing around you."

"What did you tell your four workers in the wheatfield, Philip?" asked Bartholomew.

"I just told them about what I understood of how Jesus teaches us, about the way God loves and protects us. I told them about some of the people I had seen Jesus heal. One of the men asked me why Jesus didn't heal my bad arm if he could heal other people."

"You know, I've wondered about that myself, Philip. What did you tell them?" asked Bartholomew.

"Jesus chose me the way I am because he believed I could do what he needed me to do with my stiff arm," answered Philip. "You know, Bartholomew, I think I've just discovered something! In a way Jesus really has healed my arm. Oh, I know it's still stiff and it doesn't work like the other arm, but somehow I never think about it. I do all the things I need to do. Somehow it works."

"Philip, for all your saying so often that you don't understand, I think you understand better than the rest of us." Bartholomew's eyes twinkled as he looked at his friend.

There were many years ahead for Philip. Throughout all of them he would always think of himself as the least of the disciples. In his own mind he would always have difficulty being sure he understood. There was never any doubt in his mind about Jesus, but his methodical mind wanted to be sure each step he took was the right step. Philip would never be the great leader many of the other disciples became, but he would live to prove that a follower could win people by his own example.

For Philip the trial and crucifixion of Jesus were almost unbearable. All of his faith and confidence was shaken. Jesus, the Messias, had been taken from them! What was left? He felt that he could no longer stay in Jerusalem. He would go somewhere, anywhere—anywhere but Jerusalem. Cleopas, one of those close to Jesus and the disciples, seeing that Philip was almost in a daze from grief and unhappiness, walked with him. Together they walked away from the city in the direction of Emmaus, which was only a short distance from Jerusalem. They talked as they walked, and all Philip's grief and doubts about the future came out.

As they neared Emmaus, another traveler joined them.

"Why are you so unhappy?" he asked.

"Don't you know what has happened? Are you a stranger who has just come to Jerusalem that you haven't heard all that has happened?" asked Philip bitterly.

"What things have happened?" asked the stranger.

"Then you don't know that Jesus of Nazareth, the Messias, was delivered over to the high priests and crucified!" exclaimed Cleopas.

"Jesus was the one who was to have redeemed Israel. He is

the one we knew to be the chosen one! And yet this has come to pass. It is the third day already since he was taken," added Philip, not waiting for the stranger's reply.

"Oh, you foolish ones. How slow you are to believe all that the prophets have spoken. Hasn't it been said that your Christ had to suffer these things in order to enter into his glory?" The stranger walked on with them and told them all of what the scriptures said. As they entered Emmaus, he turned aside to leave them, but Philip and Cleopas begged him to stay.

The stranger stayed with them, and they had supper together and they talked. Suddenly as they sat down together, both the disciples recognized the stranger who had walked and talked with them as Jesus. Before they could recover, he vanished from them.

Philip and Cleopas turned back toward Jerusalem, almost running in their haste to find the disciples and tell them they had seen Jesus. Now Philip the methodical thinker had the renewed strength and faith to go on. Jesus had come again! Though he would not be with them in his physical presence, just to have seen him again was enough for Philip. He could go on. The burden was not too heavy. He would go out to all the wheatfields of the world and tell about Jesus.

Go he did, to Scythia and to Phrygia. Mariamne, Philip's sister, worked with him and together they established many churches. Later in his ministry Philip's faithful friend Bartholomew joined Philip and Mariamne in Phrygia, and the three of them worked together for a time. As happened in so many cases, the governing proconsul grew jealous of the way the people responded to the teachings of Philip and Bartholomew and he had them seized. Bartholomew was released, but Philip was crucified in Hieropolis of Phrygia. Mariamne and Bartholomew took down the body from the cross and buried it tenderly. Philip the follower had learned how to lead.

BARTHOLOMEW
The Trustworthy Man

The early morning was the best time to work in the vineyard. In the early morning while the dew still was cool on the leaves the grapes seemed to respond best. The pruning went more easily at this hour. Bartholomew liked this time of the day especially. It gave him time to think and to be alone with his thoughts. Bartholomew liked being alone. It wasn't that he didn't have friends, but it was easier to think when he was by himself.

The hilly, stony soil around Cana grew grapes well, and Tholmai's vineyard was one of the best in this part of Galilee. Bartholomew, Tholmai's oldest son, was the one who cared for the vineyard. The two younger brothers looked after the sheep. As he worked, Bartholomew thought of the past month. He had gone down to the Judean desert with a group of others to listen to John the Baptizer. Word of John's preaching had spread throughout all of Palestine. The fiery tongue of the prophet was stirring many of the young men of Galilee. Bartholomew felt he must hear for himself this one they called "prophet of the wilderness." The vineyard had been well cared for and it was not the season of harvest, so Tholmai had consented to let his son go for a few days.

For two days Bartholomew listened to John and was moved by what he heard. All the long journey back to Cana he thought about what John had preached. "One comes after me whose sandal I am not worthy to touch," John had said. Bartholomew wondered when the chosen one John spoke of would make his appearance. To tell the truth, Bartholomew was a little hesitant to believe all of John's prophecies. There was no doubt John the Baptizer was a man sent by God, and a powerful preacher, but his wild appearance and fiery words made Bartholomew skeptical about how accurate all that he predicted could be.

Even so, he was glad he had gone to hear him. John was a man of conviction and courage. The words he was saying so plainly were not popular with those in Jerusalem whose power he challenged. Pilate, the governor of Judea, and Annas and Caiaphas, the high priests, did not like what they heard. Such words as "Prepare ye the way of the Lord, make his paths straight" were not pleasing to the high priests. They themselves were the high priests, the intermediary between the people and God. None should challenge their powers! The spies of the high priests and Pilate reported other words they had heard John say, such as: "I baptize you with water, but there is one mightier than I coming. I am not worthy to touch his shoes. He will baptize you with the Holy Spirit and with fire."

"The man is a dangerous madman. He is no holy prophet. What talk is this he gives the people," complained Caiaphas to Pilate. "The people will become inflamed." Pilate nodded his head. The time would come when this man would have to be dealt with.

So Bartholomew listened to the words of John and then journeyed back to Cana. At first he thought he would go back by way of Capernaum and visit with his friend Philip. He wanted to see how Philip was getting along in his new job. But thinking about it, he decided it would take too long to go by way of Capernaum. His father would be worried if Bartholomew were gone a day longer than he was expected to be away. He would try to get to Capernaum soon and visit with Philip. He'd like to see Philip's sister Mariamne as well.

Mariamne! He thought about how pretty she was. They had gotten to be good friends during the time after the storm when Philip's arm was hurt and his father had been drowned. Bartholomew heard about the storm and came down from Cana to work as a fisherman in Philip's place until his friend's arm mended. When Philip could work again, Bartholomew had helped find him a place in the shop of Tahath the sailmaker. Then Bartholomew went back to Cana to look after his father's vineyard. Back in Cana he had thought of Philip and Mariamne often. Bartholomew heaved a sigh. As soon as he could he'd go to Capernaum.

The days passed, and the weather had never been better for the grapes. There was just enough rain, and fortunately it usually fell in the morning. This was important, for when the rain came early in the day the afternoon sun dried off the leaves before the cooler night air came. This greatly accelerated the growth of the vines. They would surely have a fine crop this year. Perhaps it would make up for the crop two years past when the rains had come too late. The stony soil had dried quickly from the lack of water. Looking at the grapevines he tended with so much care, Bartholomew was satisfied. He turned and walked back down the hill toward the home where he lived with his parents, his two brothers, and his grandfather.

He did not go into the house. Instead he turned and ducked under the great spreading boughs of the fig tree which stood in front of the house. The boughs made a kind of private room. It was here Bartholomew liked to come for his own private thoughts. He was a student of the scriptures and spent much of his time thinking about what different passages meant. Some of the passages were particularly difficult. He was trying to think about a possible meaning of one passage in particular when he heard his name being called.

"Bartholomew, Bartholomew!"

Now who could that be? Bartholomew did not recognize the voice. The thick branches of the fig tree which gave him so much privacy kept him from seeing clearly who it was who called his name. Bartholomew got up and made his way out from under the tree. It was Philip! His friend from Capernaum had come!

Philip was more excited and enthusiastic than Bartholomew had ever known his friend to be. As he listened to Philip talk, Bartholomew's heart beat faster. This Jesus of Nazareth must be a wonderful person to have made cautious Philip so recklessly enthusiastic about him. Still, Nazareth was no larger than Cana. The two villages were just a few miles apart. Surely the great new leader promised by the prophets could not come from Nazareth. As well to say a king could come from Cana. Yet, who could tell? Perhaps it was possible for the chosen one to come from some small village in Galilee. Not every famous person had to come from Jerusalem or Capernaum or the other larger cities of Palestine! Yes, decided Bartholomew, he would go with his friend Philip to see this new teacher.

Along the way he thought of something. "Philip, do you know if your Jesus of Nazareth ever went to hear John the Baptizer preach?" asked Bartholomew.

"Yes, I know he went and heard John the Baptizer. Andrew and John met Jesus there and talked with him. John the Baptizer baptized Jesus. At first John the Baptizer refused to do so because he felt he was unworthy of such an honor, but Jesus insisted. Andrew told me he heard John the Baptizer call Jesus the lamb of God," answered Philip.

Bartholomew thought of John the Baptizer's words again: "One comes after me whose sandals I am not worthy to touch." They hurried on to meet Jesus. In future days, after he had become one of the twelve, Bartholomew remembered how he had doubted John the Baptizer's prophecies. If he had only stayed a few more days he might have met Jesus so much sooner. But he hadn't stayed those days. Even when he had heard John the Baptizer proclaim that one would soon come after him who would be the savior of Israel, Bartholomew hadn't been sure. How fortunate he was to have a friend like Philip, thought Bartholomew. If it had not been for Philip he might never have met Jesus! It would be hard to repay his friend for giving him the chance to meet Jesus. And then Bartholomew had been chosen to become one of the twelve. Bartholomew would always remember what Philip had done for him.

Now he was a man well past middle age, though his dark hair still showed no gray. He still had the build of a man who had worked hard and whose hands knew the grip of the pruning hook and the plowshare. For years he had labored in India, in Chaldea, in Ethiopia, bringing the good news of the teachings of Jesus to all the people. This was what Jesus had charged all of the twelve to do, and so Bartholomew did his best. Now word had come to him that he was needed in Phrygia. Another of the disciples labored there and had need of help. Bartholomew was glad to go. It would be good to see Philip again—Philip and Mariamne. The years between had been so long.

His journey was almost over, for he had come to Hieropolis in Phrygia. Now he had only to seek directions to the house where

Philip and Mariamne lived. He wondered if he had changed much. Would Mariamne recognize him? In his mind he saw the picture of a slim young girl with jet black hair and brown eyes that laughed when she talked. For a man who had traveled so far, Bartholomew carried little in the way of luggage—only a small pack strapped to his back. His wants had always been few, and it was his habit on the rare occasions when he had more than one cloak to give the other one to someone who needed it more than he.

The house was modest but neatly kept. Bartholomew sighed; it looked much like the house he remembered in Cana, but there was no fig tree with its spreading boughs before the door. He knocked again, and then it slowly opened. Bartholomew gazed at the mature woman who opened the door. Yes, Mariamne had changed, but she was still slim and beautiful. The eyes still laughed when she talked.

"Mariamne, it is I, Bartholomew."

"Bartholomew, welcome to our house! It's been so long." Mariamne threw her arms around him and drew him close to her. "Philip is here but resting now. He has not been well. He works so hard. I help all I can, but your presence will be the medicine to make him well and strong again. Come in, old friend. Come in."

It was as Mariamne had predicted. With his old friend by his side Philip regained his strength. Together the two disciples and Mariamne worked hard to establish new churches. There was opposition from the Jewish leaders. Many of them felt that the Jews of Phrygia were already too careless in the strict observance of the Temple law. A church which spoke of the brotherhood of all men and not only admitted Gentiles, but welcomed them as well, was not to their liking. The proconsul of Hieropolis, like Roman officials throughout the Empire, frowned on any religious activity which brought about controversy.

Still the disciples persisted in their work. Before their time, Paul had preached and worked in parts of Phrygia. He had not reached

Hieropolis in the lush Lycus Valley. Nor had John reached this part of Phrygia, though he had preached in other parts before going to Ephesus. With Bartholomew's help the work moved forward. Bartholomew was the more eloquent, the better orator of the two. But Philip had established himself as the head of the Christian Church in Hieropolis. He went everywhere, talking with people as they worked in the fields and vineyards. With Mariamne at his side he tended the sick, and as more people turned to the comfort of his teaching, the persecution of the new church increased.

The proconsul ordered both Philip and Bartholomew seized. They were imprisoned for many days, and each day Mariamne visited them. At last Bartholomew was released, and Mariamne and Bartholomew felt new hope that Philip would also be released. It was not to be. The persecutors of the new church demanded their victim, and they had chosen Philip.

The people of Hieropolis who had been Philip's followers were incensed by his death. The Christian movement rallied and became stronger than ever. The proconsul dared not move against them for fear of causing more turmoil than ever. Bartholomew carried on the work for a while, but finally the time came when he felt he must move on. Albanopolis in Armenia needed help, and the Christian leaders there had asked for him to come to them. He went to Mariamne to tell her.

"It is time for me to carry the word of God to other places, Mariamne. Will you come with me?" asked Bartholomew.

Slowly Mariamne shook her head. "No, Bartholomew. My place is here. I'll try to carry on the work that you and Philip have done. I can work with the poor and help tend the sick. This has become home to me. There was a time long ago when I dreamed dreams, like any girl in Galilee dreams, but that was long ago. Do not think by saying such I mean that I am sad. All of us dream dreams, but our realities mean more than dreams. You go on to Albanopolis and do the work that you must do. I'll stay here, but there will be times, when the sky turns a certain shade of blue, I'll think of Galilee and all the things that might have been." She smiled. Bartholomew returned her smile and walked away.

The work had been hard. It was always hard and the pattern did not change. Though he could not see far in this small, windowless cell, Bartholomew's eyes reached beyond the walls around him. He saw the new churches he had been able to help start. He saw a roadside in Cana of Galilee and a man seated there surrounded by his friends. Once more he could see the steady eyes look into his. Again he could hear the words he had heard so long ago: "Behold an Israelite in whom there is no guile." Bartholomew smiled to himself. He had tried to keep the trust Jesus had given him.

Already he could hear the footsteps approaching his cell. His work was finished. Soon he'd be joining the others who had gone on before. He wondered how many of them were left. There could not be many now. Perhaps only John still lived. He was not sure.

From Hieropolis he had gone to Albanopolis, and his work had met with much success. The people listened when he told them of how Jesus had come to bring the good news of God's love for all people. He told them he was one of the twelve chosen by Jesus to take his teachings to all people everywhere. Bartholomew had healed many of the sick. His fame spread throughout the surrounding country. And then the old fears and jealousies had brought on the persecution the new church always seemed to suffer. So Bartholomew was in a prison cell.

The sound of the approaching footsteps grew louder. It could only mean the time had come for him to die. He wondered what kind of death the proconsul had chosen for him. He hoped for the cross.

The cell door clanged open. Bartholomew looked up at the bulky man who almost filled the open doorway of his cell.

"Is it to be the cross?" Bartholomew asked.

The soldier in the doorway shook his head. He pointed to his companion just outside the cell. The other soldier lifted the large sword he carried so Bartholomew could see the heavy two-edged blade. The small procession walked through the narrow corridor. Bartholomew wondered if the sky was blue in Hieropolis and if Mariamne still dreamed her dreams.

JUDAS
The Man Who Could Not
Find Himself

The day was burning hot even for this small, dusty town in southern Judea. Not a breath of air stirred the leaves of the few stunted trees. It was as if no breeze dared venture into these narrow, rock-strewn valleys.

The young man working at the bench, his back to the open doorway of the shop, wiped the perspiration from his brow. He seemed intent on his work but in reality his mind was somewhere else. His thoughts were miles from this rude shop with its ever-present stench of curing hides and lime. His mouth set itself in a grim line. He slashed at the leather with the knife in his hand as if to give vent to his feelings. Intent on the stirrup strap he worked on, he did not hear the soft footsteps approaching.

"Not yet finished! What do you do with your time? What a clumsy, idle fellow you are!" The nagging words and the whining voice took the young workman by surprise. His hand slipped. With an exclamation of disgust he threw down his knife and turned toward the door.

"You startled me, father. I'll soon be through. This leather has not been well tanned. It is too stiff to cut properly." The young man—for seventeen was a man's age in Kerioth—turned again to his work.

The stooped, gray-bearded man in the doorway shuffled nearer the workbench. "This leather is good enough for a Roman. He'll pay little enough, if he pays at all. A curse on all oppressors!"

"Trinus will pay! If I must work in this stink and for a Roman at that, I'll collect what's due." The young man stood up from his work and faced the older man.

"That pride of yours will get you in trouble one day, Judas. Too good to tan hides and work leather like your father, are you? Well, you'd better get other things out of your mind, my boy. Your mother's not here to fill your head with her grand ideas. You're Judas, son of Simon the tanner of Kerioth. That's who you are and that's who you'll die! Get on with your work. My poor back is killing me, I must rest." Simon hobbled across the room of the shop to the sleeping quarters beyond.

The look on Judas' face was grimmer than ever, but he bent over his work. At last the stirrup was finished. There was more work to do but he walked to the door. Even though the air was stifling hot, he breathed in deeply. Somehow he had to get away from all this.

He was still standing in the doorway when Trinus, the Roman official in charge of the village of Kerioth, rode up calling for his stirrup. Judas hurried to lace the new stirrup strap to the saddle gear. Trinus watched, and when the stirrup had been secured, he handed over five silver shekels. Judas looked at the money in his hand. He had expected more. For all his brave words to his father Judas said nothing. The beefy Roman thrust his foot in the stirrup and swung himself up. Then the trouble began.

Trinus' full weight was in the stirrup, for it was the left one which had just been replaced. Suddenly the leather gave way. The official sprawled in the dust, his left hand still clutching the reins of his rearing horse. Slowly Trinus arose. Without a word he dropped the reins over his horse's head so they trailed in the dust and the horse stood still. Trinus turned toward Judas and his right arm flashed out. The heavy fist knocked Judas head over heels. In a moment the Roman jerked Judas to his feet. A second time the blow struck home, and again Judas lay in the dust. His cheek was swollen and cut. Trinus stretched out his fingers and looked at the blood staining the heavy ring he wore. Slowly he wiped away the blood on his sleeve.

"I'll be back in the morning, early. Work the night through if need be, but have a new stirrup in perfect condition ready for me. Otherwise there will be a bloody face to match that ugly red hair on your head." With a bound Trinus was in the saddle, riding away from the tanner's shop.

Judas picked himself up. He touched his cheek and winced as his fingers felt the bruise. He had been treated as a dog, as something less than human. This would never happen to him again. Never again would he pick up the tanner's knife—never again! Slowly he walked inside the shop and sank on the stool by the workbench. Holding his head in his hands, he thought back over the years in Kerioth.

He remembered his mother. How kind and gentle she had been. He never knew what circumstance brought her to his father. Some family misfortune must have caused her to turn to this whining, childless widower so much older than herself. Why had she married Simon, who plied his tanner's trade on the edge of the village where the smell of his trade would not offend the neighbors? Hannah was far above her husband in social position, education, and in her dreams for their only child, Judas. She had insisted on the name Judas, which meant "Praised of God." The great hero, Judas Maccabeus, had won victories in Judea. Someday *her* Judas would be as famous. She knew he would! So, as soon as her son was old enough to understand, she told him the old stories—stories of the glory of Israel and the heroes of their people.

He too would be a man people would look up to—a scribe or perhaps a rabbi. Hannah dreamed dreams and she shared them with her son. She taught him to read and to write, and there was no *hazzan* in any synagogue who taught more fiercely than Hannah taught Judas. But whatever his mother contributed to the boy's happiness, his father took from him. The boy's first recollection of his father was a whining old man complaining of his misfortune, his ill health, his hard lot. Simon of Kerioth was never satisfied, never happy.

Slowly Judas got up from the stool. He knew he would never again touch his knife to a piece of leather. Trinus could beat him until he was dead before he got a stirrup from the hand of Judas. But why stay and be beaten? Why follow a trade he hated for the benefit of a father he did not love? All that bound him to Kerioth was gone the day his mother died. He would leave! He had five silver shekels in his pocket and he knew where there were more. Surely he had earned the money.

In the next room his father slept. The empty wineskin on the floor beyond the old man's drooping arm said plainly his sleep would be deep and long. Judas placed his few belongings in the leather bag he himself had made. He girded his cloak with the long, narrow, woven leather belt he had fashioned with his own hands. Quickly he knelt by the wooden chest at his father's bed. He lifted the chest and slid back the secret panel in the bottom. He had discovered the panel long ago, but Judas had never opened it before. He removed a small leather pouch and counted more than three hundred denarii! Surely a month's wages would be little enough for the years he had labored without pay. He counted out thirty denarii and replaced the rest. It would be enough. He returned his father's treasure to its hiding place.

From the workbench he snatched a piece of smooth leather and found a bit of chalk. On the leather he wrote a message to his father: "I have taken thirty denarii—one month's wages for the years I have labored without pay. I leave Kerioth forever. The five silver shekels are payment by Trinus for the stirrup which is still not made. The first I made for him was faulty." He signed his name and placed the leather and the five silver shekels on the table near his father's bed.

He was no thief, Judas told himself. He had taken what was justly his, wages he had more than earned. The silver shekels of the Roman Trinus were left behind. His father could earn them or return them as he chose. Judas walked away from the house which had once been a home without looking back.

For a foot traveler the road was long and weary through the winding valleys of Judea, but time went quickly for Judas. Every step brought him closer to the place he had always longed to see—Jerusalem. Each year, he recalled, his mother had urged Simon to make the Passover journey, but each year her husband found some new excuse to avoid the expense of the trip. Judas had never before been beyond Kerioth. He shivered with excitement at the thought of seeing Jerusalem.

Ten miles of steady walking brought him in sight of Hebron. Walking through Hebron, he followed the road out of the city toward Bethlehem, some thirteen or fourteen miles to the northwest. Soon he found himself approaching a company of salt transporters bound for Jerusalem with salt from the Dead Sea. This was their regular route. Several times a year they made the journey from

Jerusalem to the Dead Sea. Loading their donkeys with baskets of salt, they returned to Jerusalem by way of Hebron and Bethlehem. They welcomed another strong young back to help in the loading and unloading. In return they offered a plate at the evening campfire and the protection of their company. It was a bargain Judas was glad to make.

Jerusalem

The early morning sun turned the city to gold as it did each dawn. Though he had seen the sunrise many times during these past six years, Judas never tired of the scene. To watch the first strong rays of the sun reflect off the yellow limestone buildings was a thrilling sight. Peering out of the small, slitted window of his room on the top floor of the house of old Elias, the silk merchant, Judas smiled.

Six years ago he had been an innocent from Kerioth, a country fellow gazing at the Golden City and understanding none of it. By good fortune and great frugality he had walked the thirty miles from Kerioth to Jerusalem without spending even one of his thirty denarii. The odds against a country fellow retaining such a sum safely for even a night in Jerusalem were heavy. And yet none of the many sharp-eyed, quick-fingered vagabonds, who made the narrow streets of Jerusalem so hazardous for the unwary, laid a finger on Judas. Something quite different had happened.

Pausing at the narrow window to linger over the glory of the new day's beginning, Judas recalled the incident as if it were yesterday. He had left his friends of the salt caravan soon after they entered the western gate. With so much to see he wandered aimlessly, until he found himself in a street lined on both sides with shops. One shop in particular had attracted him—the silk merchant's shop where the beautifully dyed silks flashed a rainbow of colors. Never had he seen such beauty. He could not resist going over and fingering the beautiful lengths, artfully arranged to catch the eye. The owner of the shop was busy with a customer and Judas admired each new color and design his eye chanced on. Though he did not know it, the silk was worth its weight in gold. From the corner of his eye he saw another who admired silks as well. The newcomer stood near the front of the shop. Suddenly Judas became aware that a length of purple silk was slowly disappearing up the sleeve of the man as if drawn by magic. The left arm of the stranger hung straight down, but steadily the handsomest silk in the shop was disappearing up the wide sleeve.

With a bound Judas grabbed the surprised thief and pinned both arms. A short length of purple silk hung free of the sleeve and betrayed the stranger's intent. Before Judas could say a word, the old silk merchant was by his side.

"Hold him a moment longer, friend, and then you may release him." Smiling, the silk merchant gently pulled the length of stolen silk from the sleeve of the glaring thief. Slowly the shining purple rippled free of the sleeve. At the very end was a tiny fishhook attached to a very long cord. Carefully the silk merchant removed the fishhook from the corner of the silk. At last fishhook and cord lay on the floor beneath the merchant's broad foot.

"Now, let him go. He'll not try that trick in this shop soon again." The silk merchant stepped back and Judas released his hold. The man he had held darted into the crowd and was lost.

"You've done me a great service. What can I do in return? I am Elias, a silk merchant, as you can see. I like to think this shop offers the finest silks in all of Israel."

96

"My name is Judas, just arrived in Jerusalem from Kerioth. I was attracted to your shop by the beautiful colors. I've never seen such beauty before. I felt that I had to touch them. Suddenly I saw the purple silk disappearing up that fellow's sleeve like magic. I couldn't move at first, and then I realized he must be stealing it somehow, so I stopped him."

"No shouting for help, just direct action, eh! A man of decision with a keen eye and a steady hand! These qualities can be useful to a man in my position, Judas. The trick was simple enough. A thin cord ran up the right-hand sleeve, across the shoulders through a loop in his tunic, and down the left-hand sleeve. At the end was a tiny fishhook. Clever fingers placed the hook in a corner of the cloth and the fingers of the right hand tugged the silk up the opposite sleeve, palming the cord in the right hand. I've lost more than one length of silk that way."

"I'm glad I caught him." Judas turned to go.

"Wait." Elias caught Judas by the arm. "What work have you done, Judas?"

"I worked for my father in Kerioth, tanning hides and doing leather work. I left because I hated it. I'll search until I can find another job or learn a new trade."

"Silk is far removed from leather, but a young man with brains can learn one trade as well as another. Can you read and write? Do you know how to figure sums and keep accounts?"

"I can read and write, and I kept all the accounts for my father and collected all payment for our work. We had no school in Kerioth but my mother taught me many things." Judas turned to go, his head held high and his back stiff.

"Wait, Judas of Kerioth. Take no offense at my questions. You're a stranger in Jerusalem, you say? I think I can help you. Do me the honor to dine with me? Sit over there until it is time to close the shop. Surely you'll want to rest for a bit." The smile of Elias

97

and his pleasant tone soothed Judas' ruffled feelings. He was glad of the chance to rest and the invitation to supper.

So the young man from Kerioth and the old silk merchant had dined. Without seeming to ask questions Elias had gradually unfolded Judas' life story before the evening was over. He insisted that Judas spend the night with him. Elias was a widower. His only son had died as a child. He was alone. His only relative was a brother in Capernaum.

So Judas spent the night. The next morning Elias asked him to stay in his home and work in the shop. He needed an assistant; he was growing old. Judas agreed and Elias treated him as a son, teaching him all he knew about the silk trade and many other things as well. Judas had worked hard and faithfully. His quick mind picked up the skill of trading with ease. He loved his work and was happy.

All these things passed through his mind as he gazed through the window. Judas' heart was light. Only a few weeks ago Elias had hinted he was growing weary of the daily routine of the shop. Perhaps he would retire soon to his country place a few miles from Jerusalem. The words were left unsaid, but the meaning was clear to Judas. Soon it might be Judas, the silk merchant— seller of the finest silks in Jerusalem.

He was surprised to find Elias already in the shop. In recent years the old man had left to Judas the opening of the shop in preparation for the day's business. He had given himself the luxury of a later hour of rising. It was clear Elias had something on his mind. Judas' heart beat faster. Perhaps today Elias would say: "Judas, I am retiring from this business. Take it and run it as your own. From the profits you may pay me the sum we will agree upon. I hand it on to you as I would have handed it to the son who died so long ago." Judas was sure this was what Elias was trying to bring himself to say. At last Elias called him into the back room. He seated himself across the table from Elias.

98

"I have received bad news from Capernaum," Elias began. "My brother is dead. His widow writes that my brother was unwell these last few years. His business suffered. Now there is nothing left for her or my nephew. I am sending for them both. My brother's son is only a year or two younger than you. He will take over the business here when I retire soon. It's a good business, Judas. I will double your wages. Your place will be secure here. For a time I thought things might be different. I did not know of my brother's troubles. No words have passed between us for many years." Elias stopped. He seemed to search for words without finding them.

When he spoke, Judas' voice was cool and even. "I will be gone within the hour. Just the wages which are due me; that's all I want." He left the room to pack his belongings. Only his face could not conceal the bitterness of his disappointment. Soon he returned and Elias spoke to him again.

"Do not leave, Judas. You have been treated like a son and my affection for you is unchanged. Understand that I have no choice in this matter. I must provide for my brother's family."

"I am grateful for your kindness to me, Elias, but everything is changed. There is nothing more for me here. I'll take my wages and be off." Judas held out his hand palm upward.

Elias counted out a generous settlement—more than twice the wages which were due. "You'll make your mark, Judas. No doubt of it. As a friend I give you this advice: too much ambition rides heavy on the back of any man. When the desire to be first goads you too keenly, remember—a man can lose a prize and still win the world." Elias smiled sadly, holding both hands outstretched in a gesture of friendship.

Judas merely shook his head. "No man can win the world by losing," he said. Head held high he strode through the doorway. Elias followed looking after him, but Judas never looked back.

One of the Twelve

The marketplace of Capernaum was a busy place. Caravans from Damascus and Syrian Antioch brought goods in great abundance to the merchants of Galilee. Though the town was busy, it lacked the glamor and sophistication of Jerusalem. Judas smiled as he walked the streets, but it was not a happy smile. He missed the shop of Elias. He missed the pageantry of the great Temple and the clamor of the Temple crowds. There was nothing in all of Galilee to compare with the Golden City.

Judas had saved his money carefully during the years he had worked with Elias, and the old man's generous settlement had added to his store of funds. He could afford to take his time in making a new connection, a place where his talents would be recognized and appreciated. Something that offered a real opportunity, that's what he was looking for. Even now he had discovered a possibility. A friend from Jerusalem was stopping at the same inn. They had dined together. His friend had hinted to Judas at a great undertaking where the stakes were high and the rewards worth the risk. Judas had been shrewd enough to show interest but to ask no questions. He was meeting his friend again this evening. The hour of their meeting was close at hand. He hastened his pace.

The hour was late but Judas could not sleep. The excitement of the evening kept him wide awake. His friend from Jerusalem (even here alone in his room Judas dared not breathe his name) spent much of the evening finding out how Judas felt about a number of things. When Judas related the story of how he left Kerioth and the incident with Trinus, his face turned red with anger. Without thinking, his hand fingered the scar on his face where the ring of Trinus had left its mark. Almost at once his friend had begun to talk more openly.

Slowly Judas became aware that there were men in Galilee organized and ready to take chances. Men who wanted to see this land, where Moses had led and Joshua had conquered, free from the Roman rule. The old excitement swept over him. The scar on his cheek burned like a flame. He had agreed to the oath of secrecy without hesitation. There were too many men like Trinus throughout this land. It was time somebody brought them down. The Zealots, for that is what the fierce group who hoped to overthrow the Romans were called, would do it! Judas would be one of them! Here was a chance that offered more than a shopkeeper's wage.

At first Judas was given small responsibilities—locating a meeting place here, carrying a message there. Gradually his gift for organization was noticed. Someone began to see that the new member was a skillful trader. No one could bargain for a price as well as he. Soon Judas was placed in charge of buying supplies for the movement. With his trade connections he could move about the marketplace without creating any notice, and whatever he bought was always purchased at the lowest price available. Somewhat later he was given a position of greater trust as a discreet solicitor of funds for the Zealot cause.

The good name of Elias opened many doors to his former employee. As a result of his one-time connection with Elias he met Matthias, the leading silk merchant of Capernaum. Matthias welcomed a trained helper who had held a responsible position as assistant to Elias. For Judas the opportunity was twofold: working with Matthias provided an income and the opportunity to make contacts for the Zealots. With all his activity Judas still was unhappy. Gradually he began to see that his only worth to the Zealots was as a quartermaster and keeper of small funds. There would

101

be no power for him in this role. He could see that the Zealots were fierce nationalists intent on overthrowing the Romans but with no notion of how to take power and rule. They had no single leader around whom the people would rally.

Judas turned his attention to Matthias, but here also there was no opportunity. Matthias had young sons and a trusted second in command. For Judas there was a living wage, but nothing more. Somewhere there must be a chance for him to fulfill his destiny! Somewhere there was a leader he could follow, one who could use and appreciate his talents.

Judas made a decision. The Zealots were madmen rushing in all directions. Though he hated the Romans as much as the Zealots did, Judas was wise enough to see the road they traveled led only to defeat. He had had enough of that. No, there was no future with the Zealots. Perhaps the way to greatness lay in another direction.

This Jesus, the Nazarene, wrought quiet miracles. Water into wine at a wedding feast, sick people healed. Then there had been the awesome sight at the Temple itself. Judas would not have believed any man would turn over the tables of the money changers and speak so sternly to the priests. But Judas had witnessed the whole affair with his own eyes.

He had returned to Jerusalem not with the thought of reconciling himself with Elias or embarking on a new business venture. He had come because he was completely caught up in following this man who had so captured his imagination. Jesus, who spoke of love as the way to conquer but who had used force to turn out from the Temple those who abused the name of God. At first Judas had been shocked, and then his shock had turned to fierce delight. Here was a man who knew when to speak softly and when to act boldly. Here was a man to follow!

Gradually as he followed Jesus and his followers from place to place, Judas struck up a speaking acquaintance with a few of them. It was Andrew he approached first, telling him he wanted to speak with Jesus. Andrew brought the Judean to Simon.

"Why does a Judean seek the company of Galileans?" asked Simon, speaking bluntly as usual.

"Your Master does not speak of Judeans or Galileans. When I listen to him he speaks of *all* men—a new way of life for all men; a new kingdom coming for *all* men, or did I not hear rightly?" Judas spoke coldly to the brawny older brother of Andrew and looked him straight in the eye.

"No, you heard rightly. The Master has said those words and he teaches all men are equal. Follow along if you must, but don't bother Jesus or the rest of us. If he wants to meet and talk with you, he'll tell one of us." Simon turned away.

"He doesn't mean to sound so hard, Judas. That's Simon's way. He loves the Master and thinks only to protect him. There are many who follow us now. The Master cannot speak to each person. You understand?" Andrew smiled and clasped Judas' hand in his.

Judas did not take the rough words of Simon lightly. They had stung, and Judas was a proud man. Nevertheless he determined to continue. In his heart and mind Judas was convinced that Jesus was the one person who could build a new kingdom. Already the crowds were growing. People were following everywhere. More and more the name Jesus of Nazareth was on the lips of all of Galilee. There were eyes in Judea who watched as well. Judas would follow. Sooner or later there would be a place for him.

He was very tired. All day he had walked, and now late in the evening the way led uphill, around the lower slope of Mount Tabor. Surely they would not climb all the way to the top. Still Jesus continued to walk on with the five who were always near him. Judas trailed far behind with perhaps a hundred other followers. At last those in front prepared to make camp. They had come to a level place extending across the whole top of the hill. The heights of Mount Tabor rose above them.

Judas was too exhausted to sit around the fire and share the common supper, as had become the custom of those who followed Jesus at a distance. The man from Kerioth simply wrapped himself in his cloak and lay on the ground. His leather bag was his pillow. Tired as he was, sleep did not come quickly. Perhaps he had been wrong. Perhaps there was no place for him in this company. His money was almost gone, his clothes were becoming worn. He was thankful he had purchased new sandals on his return from Jerusalem. Tomorrow he would decide. It might be best to turn back to Capernaum and find a place in one of the shops of the marketplace. He had followed so many dreams, only to see them vanish when he felt they were ready to come true. The bitterness of his thoughts kept him awake for a long time, but toward morning Judas slept.

The sun was up. On the edge of the crowd Judas awoke. Slowly he rubbed the sleep from his eyes and looked around. He turned his back on the crowd and gathered his belongings. He paused only to adjust the strap on the leather bag. It was the old bag which has been on his back when he left Kerioth. How many miles since Kerioth? Too many to remember, too many useless miles following too many useless dreams. He started to walk away.

"Judas, Judas of Kerioth!" It was Andrew who called. Judas turned as he saw Andrew running toward him.

"Judas, the Master wants to talk with you. I've been sent to bring you to him." Andrew stood before Judas, a little out of breath but smiling.

"You mean he asked to speak to *me?* He asked for me by name? How does he know me?" Judas could feel his heart pounding against his ribs. He wanted to turn and run up the hill toward Jesus, and yet he was puzzled and afraid.

"He asked for you by name. I was told to go fetch Judas of Kerioth. The Master is choosing some of us, only twelve I think, to work closely with him. Perhaps you will be one, Judas."

"How many has he chosen thus far, Andrew?" Judas frowned anxiously.

"I don't know how many have been chosen. My brother Simon, James, Matthew, John, and even me—perhaps Philip and Thomas. I've seen Jesus talking to them and others. Come on, let's hurry, Judas." Andrew started back the way he had come.

Judas continued to hesitate. He wanted desperately to follow Andrew but he was afraid. He was afraid of being disappointed. Suppose Jesus talked to him and decided against choosing him. Judas looked around. There must be five hundred people here now. Only twelve from all this group! For a moment Judas was on the verge of turning on his heel and running down the hill. Then his self-confidence came back.

"Go on ahead, Andrew. I'll follow. I want to make myself as presentable as I can." Quickly Judas shook out the wrinkles from his cloak. Carefully he brushed away the dust and grass as best he could. From a neighbor he begged a cup of water and dabbed at his face. He adjusted his headdress. Only a few stray red curls escaped. He was ready. Heart pounding, legs shaky, Judas climbed the hill toward Jesus.

"Sir, I am Judas of Kerioth. Andrew told me you wanted to speak to me." Judas stood before Jesus, who was seated on a large boulder.

"Why do you follow us, Judas?" The voice was low but of such a quality that it carried easily. The speaker's smile was friendly and compelling. Judas could not turn his eyes away.

"You are the new leader. Soon all the people will follow you," answered Judas honestly. "I have never seen people follow anyone as the crowds seek you. See, since last night the crowd has increased four times over, and still they come."

"The way will not be easy. The crowds may not always be here. There are many hard truths to learn. Not all will listen. Not all who hear will believe."

Judas dropped to the ground as he listened to the words Jesus spoke. Yes, he thought, there *will* be hard days ahead. When a new leader replaces those already in power, there are hard truths to learn. There were plenty who would not listen to a new voice and there were many who would oppose any new leadership.

"What you say is true, Master. I understand and accept it. The way I have come has not been easy. I understand hardship and can endure it. I have made my own way. I know I can serve you and your cause well."

"We go armed with love, Judas. This is our only weapon to conquer the hearts and minds of men. It is all we need." The calm voice and the steady eyes held Judas in a vise.

It was true. The Master needed no army of Zealots. Wherever he went he won the hearts of the people. They loved him instantly. A man with power to heal the sick; a man with courage to chase the money changers out of the Temple and to challenge the priests—such a man could do anything.

"If I am granted the honor to serve in your company, I will serve well and with all my skill." Judas stood up. There was nothing more he could say.

"Serve with all your love, Judas. Skill is easier learned than love. You will be one of the twelve."

His head fairly bursting with excitement, Judas heard only the last words, *"You will be one of the twelve."* He had a new dream to follow! He made his way to Andrew and the others. In a daze he looked around the group where he stood. Andrew came over and grasped his hand. As he looked around, it came over Judas. There were twelve of them in the group. He had become the twelfth disciple. He had been the last one chosen. For a moment he frowned, but then the pride of being one of the twelve came over him. The Master himself had been born in Bethlehem of Judea. Let them call Jesus a Nazarene if they wished. They were

Judeans—one from Bethlehem, one from Kerioth—only two among these Galileans.

The days that followed were days of wonder and learning for Judas. Now he was always close to Jesus. Before he had watched from a distance. Now with his own eyes he actually saw sick people healed, blind people regain their sight. At Nain when the young son of the widow had been restored to life at a word from Jesus, Judas' joy knew no bounds. There was nothing his new leader could not do.

It was the next day that Judas drew Simon Zelotes as his partner when Jesus sent them out in pairs to preach the word and heal the sick. They left with no money—only the clothes on their backs —but they were welcomed and given food and shelter at each village where they stopped.

The mission was a golden opportunity for Judas to show his real talent for presenting this new cause effectively. His eyes shone when he related the deeds he had seen Jesus perform. Judas could speak with conviction, and often he persuaded people of wealth to make a contribution. Simon Zelotes sought out the ill and the dying to help and to comfort. His work was among the poor while Judas sought to gather those leaders among the villages and talk to them about Jesus, the new leader.

He told Simon Zelotes of the contributions he had collected. Simon was impressed, but doubtful that Judas should have accepted the money.

"They want to give, Simon. Many of these people have more than enough to share. They may not get a chance to see Jesus or hear him, but they can help in this way." Judas was impatient with Simon for not understanding the importance of having a treasury.

"Well, you make it sound all right, Judas, but I don't know whether Jesus will like it or not. He may wonder why they don't share what they have with the poor of their own villages." Gentle

Simon Zelotes wanted no argument with his friend, but he was doubtful that his Master would approve.

The day to reassemble had arrived. Both the disciples were glad to rejoin Jesus and the others. Simon Zelotes wanted to tell of the sick he had healed in Jesus' name. Judas was anxious to show the Master how many people had proved their belief in his leadership through their contributions. It was all very well to talk, but money proved when people believed in a new cause.

When his turn came, Judas opened the leather bag he carried and spread the money on the ground. Proudly he waited for the words of commendation he was sure he would hear. The response was different than he had anticipated.

Instead of praising him the Master merely smiled his strange smile, which was neither merry nor sad. He inquired if they had obtained lodging and food without difficulty. Standing beside Judas, Simon the Zealot answered that all doors were opened to them. Judas spoke up quickly: "Master, all I have gathered is here. We have not spent even one of the coins collected."

Then Jesus spoke, and his words indicated that perhaps they had no need of the money since the villagers had freely offered food and lodging.

"Not for ourselves but for the company, for the cause—this is why I accepted the money which was given." Judas could not understand why the Master failed to see the importance of accumulating funds of some kind. Somebody in this company had to be practical. His disappointment gave way to satisfaction when it was he who was chosen to be steward of the treasury. Judas had feared Matthew would be chosen, but the former tax collector had refused to have anything to do with money. Simon had proposed Matthew and Judas had hidden his resentment. Then when Matthew had refused to be considered, Andrew proposed Judas, and Simon the Zealot supported him. So Judas became treasurer.

The next day they traveled from Capernaum to Bethsaida. Still the crowds followed them even into the hills outside the city. Here something took place which made a great impression on Judas. It was late in the day, and Jesus continued to speak to the people of love for each other and a new way of life. At last Simon reminded Jesus the hour was late and the people would have difficulty reaching their homes in time for the evening meal. Jesus asked if any in the crowd had brought food with them. The disciples could find only one small boy who had a few dried fish and a few small loaves of bread.

At Jesus' suggestion the disciples divided the crowd into groups of about fifty. Then he told them to take the loaves and the fishes and break them into pieces and pass them among the people. As they did this, there was always enough left for the next person. Even when all had eaten there were fragments enough left over to fill several baskets. These were gathered to distribute to the poor. Judas marveled at what had happened. No wonder Jesus had not been impressed with the modest collection he had accumulated. It would have been as easy to feed an army as to have fed this huge gathering. He had never seen any miracle as practical as this one. Surely the day was coming when Jesus would assert his full power. When that day came he would need a man like Judas—a practical man.

A Hill Outside Jerusalem

Judas got along well with the other disciples, though he and Simon-bar-Jonah had no real affection for each other and kept their distance. Simon-bar-Jonah was blunt and said exactly what he felt. Judas had the feeling that Simon-bar-Jonah never really trusted him. For his part Judas could never understand why the Master always seemed to give preference to Simon. For all of that, things went along well enough until, for Judas, the worst possible thing happened.

The day had begun as usual. The disciples busied themselves about the camp. Jesus was alone, praying in the early morning. When the simple breakfast was prepared, John went to bring the Master to the group so that they might begin. After they had eaten Jesus motioned to them to remain seated. He wished to talk to them.

"Who do men say the Son of God is?" he asked them. The various answers came from first one and then another.

"John the Baptizer . . . Elijah . . . Jeremias."

"But who do *you* say that I am?"

As Judas listened to the question Jesus asked, he quickly formed the answer he would give. He would say: "You are the ruler of the new kingdom and you will rule with justice over all the people of this land." He was sure that this would be a pleasing answer. Perhaps Jesus would smile and say, "Judas, you have spoken well. Of the twelve here who will help me you shall be the lord high treasurer." He smiled to himself. Best let some of the others speak first, then he would give his answer. His daydream ended abruptly with the sound of Simon-bar-Jonah's strong voice in his ears.

"You are the Christ, the Son of the living God!" The fisherman leaped to his feet, hands on his hips, as he looked up at Jesus standing above him.

Judas was glad Simon had answered first. What kind of answer was this? It wasn't really an answer at all. Surely this was one time Simon would be called down.

"Blessed are you, Simon son of Jonah, for no man has revealed

110

this truth to you, but it has been revealed to you by my Father in heaven.

"I say to you that you are Peter, and upon this rock I will build my church; and the gates of hell shall not prevail against it. And I will give to you the keys of the kingdom of heaven; and whatsoever you shall bind on earth shall be bound in heaven; and whatsoever you shall loose on earth shall be loosened in heaven."

Judas heard the words of Jesus and suffered in the hearing. Again it was Simon! Simon would be first. Simon was always first! "You are Peter, and upon this rock . . . . I will give you the keys of the kingdom." These were bitter words for Judas. The keys of the kingdom for Simon—or Peter, to give him his new name. For Judas there was nothing. Why was it always so? He had been loyal and faithful. Whatever task had been assigned to him he had carried out. The little fund for which he had been responsible had been watched with care. Not a penny had been lost or un-accounted for. When one of the group needed new sandals Judas had found the money and purchased them himself. When bread was needed Judas had bought it at the lowest price in the market. Somehow the careful management of Judas had stretched the treasury to cover every need. It did not seem fair never to be recognized, never to be praised.

Simon—Simon Peter now—had never liked Judas. If he was to be publicly acknowledged as the one next to the Master, what chance would there be for Judas? All these angry thoughts went through the mind of Judas but he managed to keep them to himself. He went about his daily duties just as always. He was more silent than before and he smiled less than ever. But then he had never smiled often. Nobody seemed to notice any difference.

Judas' spirits lifted slightly as they traveled toward Jerusalem. Surely this was the climax. If a new kingdom was coming, then Jerusalem had to be confronted. It was well enough to gain popular support among the towns and villages of Galilee, but there would be no real change in power unless Jerusalem fell under the spell of Jesus. There were still a good number of people with them, but lately there had been more spies from Jerusalem among them. Judas had kept many of the connections established during his merchant days. He heard rumors that Caiaphas, the chief priest, had warned the ruling council of the Temple to take heed of this Galilean upstart who seemed to have such a following among the people.

It was the decision to march on Jerusalem that convinced Judas. In Jerusalem were the most powerful enemies of Jesus and the twelve. Yet straight toward Jerusalem they made their way. No man went to his enemies without a plan. This was the kind of strategy that appealed to Judas. He had worried about an ambush in Samaria or a trap in Capernaum. If there was to be a face-to-face confrontation in Jerusalem, the Master would use his power to even the odds. Judas felt confident.

The pace toward the Golden City was too leisurely for Judas, but Jesus wanted to stop by Bethany and visit with an old friend. They came to the house of Lazarus, and Lazarus insisted on providing supper for all.

"This is the least that I can do," said Lazarus, smiling. "I would not be here to greet you now were it not for Jesus." His sister Mary brought out a jar of costly spikenard and anointed Jesus as they ate. Judas remarked that so costly a gift should really have been sold and the money distributed to the poor. He had made the remark half in jest, but in truth the treasury was very low. Judas always worried when the small funds they carried were almost gone. They could have used the money the ointment would have brought. Expenses in Jerusalem would be very high. Even if the ointment had been sold and the money distributed to the poor it would have been of some benefit to the company. It would have attracted the kind of favorable publicity they needed.

But again Judas had been reproved. Jesus had said Mary had

done a beautiful thing and had prepared his body for burial. He had gone on to say that the poor were always present but that he would not always be with them. Judas simply did not understand this at all. It was plain that no person was prepared for burial while he was alive. As for the poor, it was always Jesus who insisted that the poor be fed even when there was scarcely enough money to feed the twelve. How many times Judas had reluctantly counted out the last coin from the treasury to buy food for the poor at Jesus' own request. Another rebuff, another slap in the face for Judas.

Still Judas found hope. Earlier, seventy of the faithful had been sent on ahead with the message: "The harvest is plentiful, but the laborers are few; pray therefore the Lord of the harvest to send out laborers into his harvest."

The message was plain enough to Judas, even though the others seemed to attach no special significance to it. This was the signal Jesus was sending out to those of his supporters in Judea who would arise and support him at the signal. The time had come for a show of strength for Jesus.

When the seventy returned with the good news that their mission had proceeded well and they had cast out demons in the name of Jesus, Judas again found a meaning others of the twelve did not. Casting out demons surely meant the enemy spies had been uncovered and disposed of. To speak of the people receiving them well meant they were ready to rise and march toward Jerusalem.

On this day they would enter Jerusalem. The day was beautiful. Not a cloud in the sky. Even early in the morning people were coming toward them shouting and waving palm branches.

"Blessed is the King of Israel who comes in the name of the Lord!" some were shouting. Judas was very proud. He wondered if Elias or his nephew stood in the crowd. There were so many people he could not single out a familiar face. On he marched, close to the side of Jesus, who was riding on a young donkey colt. Judas kept his face straight ahead, toward Jerusalem.

Judas waited patiently for some word from Jesus. Surely there would be a meeting to plan strategy. There was a great opportunity, with the crowds surging into the city, to start something with a speech which would inflame the people. Surely something was going to happen! But the Master talked with the people in small groups in the same gentle tones. He answered their questions, and the answers were strange to Judas' ears. Much of the time Jesus seemed to wish to be alone to pray and to meditate or just be alone with his own thoughts.

The old doubts came over Judas again. After the triumphal entry into Jerusalem there had been nothing. Here had been the best chance of all. Clearly the people were with Jesus, but there had been no great speeches to bring the people rallying around, clamoring for a new leader. There had been no attack on Caiaphas and the others who, with him, ruled the Temple. The same abuses were going on as before, but the Master did not attack them. Instead Jesus hinted again of his own death. Judas became more uncertain and confused than ever.

Truly the Master had seemed to be saying that he would die and leave them. But this could not be! If this were true, then there would be no new kingdom, no glorious reforms with true justice for all. There would be no new power sweeping over Israel and putting out the Roman usurpers. There would be no new priests for the Temple. Annas and Caiaphas would be ruling the Temple and the people as well. This little band of twelve—what could they do without Jesus? Simon Peter would be in charge! Blustering Simon Peter—the rock of Galilee. Well, he was still just a fisherman as far as Judas was concerned. He was not a leader, not a planner, not a great speaker who could rally people to a dangerous cause. None of the others were much better.

There *was* one way to bring things to a head. Judas knew Jesus had the power to strike down any man. Surely one who could raise people from the dead could strike them down as well. Caiaphas was the one who held a stranglehold on the rank and file of the people. Break the hold of Caiaphas and get the people to rally around a new leader. That was the way. Then when the people rose up would be the time to put Pilate out of the way.

Judas arranged a meeting with Caiaphas. He knew the high priest would not arrest Jesus while he was surrounded by his followers. There was enough opposition to the high-handed rules Caiaphas forced on the Jewish people already. Caiaphas listened to the plan eagerly. At night the Garden of Gethsemane was a quiet place. No large crowds could assemble there. Caiaphas half-closed his eyes. What payment was being asked? Judas shrugged his shoulders carelessly—thirty silver shekels. He knew the high priest's greed would jump at concluding the bargain with so small a sum. He had a fleeting moment of anxiety. Who would sell his leader for so small a sum? Perhaps Caiaphas would smell a trap? But no, the high priest nodded his head eagerly. Judas wondered if his own worn sandals and threadbare cloak had made the small sum seem greater to the high priest. Quickly Judas left.

It was the night of the Passover supper. The twelve were together in the room Simon Peter and John had arranged. They had followed the ritual supper in the old tradition, and now it was ended. The others talked together as usual, but Judas slipped away now that the meal had been completed. It was not unusual for him to leave earlier than the rest. Often there were arrangements to be made for the next day. Sometimes there was food or a money offering to be distributed to the poor. No thought was given to his absence by the others.

Slowly the little band walked away from the upper room and over into the garden. The night was still but not cold. Jesus went apart from the others, as he often did, to pray and to think his own thoughts. Slowly in the warm air the disciples fell asleep. It was very still.

From below, along the winding paths of the garden, several

pinpoints of light bobbed and weaved upward in the darkness. None of the disciples noticed, for they were sleeping. The lights flickered and came nearer. At last they approached the corner of the garden where the disciples rested and Jesus was praying. Sleepily the disciples awakened.

It was Judas leading the way! Behind came an officer and a company of the Temple guard. At an order one of the guard stepped over to lay hands on Jesus. In an instant Simon Peter had drawn his sword and slashed out, cutting off the ear of the man. At once Jesus put out his hand and told Simon Peter to put away his sword.

The captain of the guard led Jesus away. Stunned by what had happened, the disciples scattered in all directions. Judas stole away silently with the Temple guard. Already, now that the deed had been done, Judas was having second thoughts. Had he been right in bringing about this situation where Jesus would be face to face with Caiaphas? Surely his Master had the power to demonstrate once and for all that Jesus was indeed the chosen one!

It was early morning when Judas followed the captain of the guard into the palace of Caiaphas. He stood near the rear of the room. Caiaphas made the formal charge of blasphemy. Jesus stood calmly answering in his quiet voice—too low for Judas to hear. There was no sudden miracle; no miraculous loosening of the bonds which held Jesus. Caiaphas did not fall down dead! Judas heard the words indicating Jesus would be taken before Pilate with the recommendation of Caiaphas, backed by the ruling council of the Temple, that he be crucified for the crime of blasphemy.

Dismayed and confused, Judas turned to leave the room. The coins rattled in his pocket. He reached into the pocket and flung the coins toward Caiaphas and ran from the room. Blindly he ran down the streets of Jerusalem. On and on he ran, and reached the outskirts of the city. Ahead of him was a low hill with a cluster of trees. It seemed to Judas he could never stop running. Too late he began to dimly understand some of the words he had heard so many times before without really hearing or understanding them. Perhaps he had not understood because he had tried to make them take on the meaning he had wanted them to have. They rang in his brain like the slow, solemn tones of a great bell.

"My kingdom is not of this world. . . . One of you will betray me. . . . Whither I go, you cannot follow now; but you shall follow me afterward . . . . If your brother trespasses against you, rebuke him; and if he repents forgive him. . . . Be you therefore merciful, as your Father also is merciful." The words kept repeating themselves over and over in his brain. He could scarcely see for the tears that blinded him and would not stop. He should have been panting for breath but his feet seemed to run on air. Still the words sang in his brain. "If he repents forgive him, forgive him, forgive him."

He had come well away from the city to the shelter of the small grove of trees on a hill outside Jerusalem. Quickly he unloosened the long braided leather belt he used as a girdle. He had made it with his own hands in Kerioth so long ago. How many months he had carried it in the leather bag. Then when his clothes were almost threadbare and his girdle had finally broken beyond repair, he had remembered this one. Now it would serve still once more. Quickly he flung his cloak on the ground. A few feet away was a large stone. He rolled it to the spot he selected and stood on it. Judas knotted the leather belt securely. The last words came to his lips again. "And if he repent, forgive him." The limb bent. The green leaves of the tree rippled with the sudden shock. Turning their gray undersides toward the sun, the leaves gleamed like silver.

THOMAS
Who Had the Courage to Question

Most of the shore was rocky, but there was one short stretch of sandy beach free from stones. It was here the two boys played their game. They took turns throwing their sharp-pointed sticks so they stuck firmly in the sand. First one threw his stick and then the other. The second to throw tried to knock over his opponent's stick while keeping his own upright. A passerby would surely have stopped and watched. It was not the game which would have caught a stranger's eye. Boys in Galilee had played the game of "sticks" as long as the oldest Galilean could remember. It was the boys themselves who would have been the center of attention.

The two were no more than twelve and no different from most

boys in Bethsaida, except for one thing. Each was a duplicate of the other. Not a hair on one head differed from the other. Even the two voices had the same exact intonation and sound.

"That's two for me, Eliel," one of the boys shouted as he knocked over the other's stick, keeping his own sticking in the sand.

"Now it's my turn, Judah," answered the one called Eliel. "Watch this!" With careful aim he knocked his brother's stick to the ground. He shouted with glee while his own stick quivered for a moment, leaned, but did not fall. The two boys kept on with their play until their mother's voice called them from the game.

They were the twin sons of Melech, a fisherman of Bethsaida. Melech's proudest possessions were his sons. He never grew tired of talking about his two boys who were so completely alike.

"How are the twins today, Melech?" asked Zebedee. He asked the question in fun, but Melech took it seriously.

"Fine, Zebedee. Both my boys are doing well. They learn their lessons quickly. The *hazzan* says he cannot tell one from the other. As alike as two olives on a tree, he says. Well he might say it, too. Even I can't tell one from the other. It's really remarkable, you know. Everyone says they've never seen two boys look so alike." The fisherman would have talked on, but Zebedee raised his hand.

"I know, I know. If you want bread for those remarkable sons to eat we'd best be casting off." And so the fishing fleet got under way and Melech broke off his talk to take his place at the oar. The boat moved out in the early evening dark. By the time they reached the fishing grounds the moon would be high. Now there was little light.

The hours passed, while the fishing fleet lowered their nets and strove to fill the boats with fish. On the shore in Melech's house a sudden light appeared. Rebekah, Melech's wife, had heard a voice cry out. She lit a lamp and took it to the room where her two boys lay sleeping. One boy lay quietly asleep. The other tossed and turned. The fretful boy's face was flushed. Rebekah laid her hand

119

on his head. The skin was hot to her touch. Her son had a fever. As she watched, the lad cried out but did not awaken.

Quickly Rebekah put down her lamp and left, to come back in a moment with a basin of cool water and a soft cloth. She dipped the cloth into the basin, wrung it partly dry, and placed the cool cloth on her son's forehead. Suddenly her other son sat up in bed. Rubbing the sleep from his eyes, he asked his mother, "What is wrong? Why are you here? Is something the matter with Eliel?"

"Your brother has a fever. This cloth I put on his head will help make him well. Go back to sleep." The boy who had awakened smiled at his mother, lay back upon his bed, and soon was fast asleep again.

All through the night Rebekah applied cool cloths to her son's brow. She could not break the fever. By early morning the fever seemed even higher. At last Melech returned. When he saw his son's condition, he was beside himself with worry.

"Go, husband! Take the road to Capernaum. Find a physician there and bring him back with you. Our son grows weaker and the fever will not break!" Rebekah urged her husband to the door. Melech was torn between his fear of leaving his son and his need for help. At last he left, running down the road toward Capernaum.

The hot sun of Galilee was high overhead. Melech led the physician's donkey at the best pace he could get the small animal to move. He saw the crowd around his doorstep before he reached his house. The bitter wailing from within produced a fear which clutched his heart. Holding the physician's hand in his, he pulled him through the crowd and into the house.

Rebekah raised her tear-stained face to meet her husband's. "It's too late. Our son is gone. Eliel is dead!" Her tears completed whatever more she might have said. Melech, his grief too much to bear, shouted out an oath. He sank to his knees beside the body of his son. The physician touched the lad's forehead, shook his head, and turned away.

120

The burial rites had been performed. The sad procession of family, friends, and playmates of Eliel had returned from the burial place. The house of Melech was quiet now. The sorrowing parents had been so absorbed in grief for their dead son they had almost forgotten there was another son who lived. Rebekah remembered how quiet her other son had been. He'd hardly said a word or made a sound. He needed comforting as much as she. She searched the house but could not find him. She called his name and heard no answer.

"Melech, Melech! We must find our other boy. I cannot find him anywhere. He has not said a word these past two days. It's hard to be a twin and lose a brother. Go search for the boy. We must find him and comfort him." Rebekah's heart was near to breaking as she tugged at her husband's sleeve, entreating him to hurry.

Melech roused himself from his grief. At last he understood. He searched along the shore where he knew his sons had often played. He found no sign of his lost boy. Andrew, Philip, James— none of his son's playmates had seen the lad. At last the worried father climbed the hills outside Bethsaida. There was a place where the dark basalt stone was cut by stonecutters from Capernaum. There he found his son.

The lost boy lay on his back, gazing at the sky. He made no move when his father came up to him. Melech sat beside him.

"What are you doing here, my son?" Melech asked the boy.

"This is where we sometimes came to be alone, Eliel and I. This was our secret place. I hoped if I came here he might come back to me," the boy replied.

"Eliel can't come back. You must know that," his father said.

"I think I really know he can't come back, and yet I miss him so I feel if I stay here he'll find a way to me. I would not have gone back to sleep that night except mother said he'd be all right." The boy sat up and looked at his father.

Melech picked his son up in his arms and held him close. "Your

121

mother hoped Eliel would be well. She did her best to break his fever. There was nothing more she could do. Our people accept God's will. You must accept the fact your brother is gone. Come, let's go home now. Your mother is worried." Melech walked back to the small house by the shore, his son's hand held tight in his.

The next morning Melech sought out Zebedee to tell him he was leaving Bethsaida.

"I'm leaving Bethsaida, Zebedee. We go to Capernaum. My brother is a carpenter there. I'll learn his trade. This place has too many memories for my family and for me."

And so the boy—who had been a twin—grew up and learned the carpenter's trade in Capernaum. He was a lonely boy. Somehow a part of him lay buried in Bethsaida. He grew up never understanding why his brother was taken from him. They had done everything together. In all their lives until his brother's death they had not been parted. It was hard to be a twin when one was gone.

The carpenter had nearly finished the oxen yoke on which he was working. He rubbed the inner surface carefully with the coarse stone. Lifting the stone, he ran his hand across the curve. It would lie smooth and even. He did not smile—Thomas seldom smiled—but he was satisfied. His work was good. A sudden shadow in the doorway caused him to look up.

"Thomas, I hoped I'd find you here." The pleasant voice of a man his own age greeted the carpenter from the doorway.

"Good morning, Andrew. What brings you here? A new oar, perhaps?" inquired Thomas.

"Nothing like that, Thomas. Something much more important. Do you remember when I asked you to go with John and me some weeks ago? You know, when we went to Judea to listen to John the Baptizer preach?" Andrew moved from the doorway into the shop and stood next to his friend.

122

"Yes, I remember. That was when I had six new chests to make for Matthias the silk merchant. Had it not been for that job I would have gone with you. Did you hear the Baptizer?" Thomas placed the finished yoke against the wall in a corner of the shop.

"Yes, we heard the Baptizer speak, but more than that, we met Jesus of Nazareth! Thomas, this man is the Messias! He is the one who will redeem Israel! My brother Simon, James and John and I are in his company. Matthew, the former publican, and Philip too have become his followers. He will choose only twelve to work with him as his closest friends. Come with me and meet him, Thomas. I feel sure he will choose you. Will you come?" The earnest tone of Andrew's voice made Thomas look at him thoughtfully.

"How can you be so sure? Why should the one spoken of by the prophets come from Nazareth? Nazareth is only a small village in the hills. What proof have you?" asked Thomas.

"Proof? I'm not sure I have any proof. Perhaps the only proof I have is the feeling in my own heart, but there are some things I can tell you," Andrew answered. "Let's sit down and I'll tell you some of the things I know about Jesus. First of all, while John and I listened to John the Baptizer preach we were standing close to him. The Baptizer looked at one who stood in back of us and called out, 'Behold the lamb of God.' It was Jesus of whom he spoke. As you know from what you've heard, John the Baptizer speaks only what he truly feels. He's not a man who can be fooled by false prophets.

"And there is more to tell. Jesus asked John the Baptizer to baptize him. John the Baptizer did not want to do it. He said he was not worthy, but Jesus insisted. We saw Jesus baptized there in the Jordan. Later John-bar-Zebedee and I talked with him. I've never talked with such a one as Jesus. His voice is gentle, and yet it carries authority. Somehow when Jesus points out what should be done you *want* to do it. You do not feel he commands you.

123

I'd walk through fire for him. He healed Simon's mother-in-law of a high fever with just a touch of his hand. He has healed others, too. Many others. He *is* the Messias, Thomas. I know he is!"

"With a touch of his hand Jesus cured the mother-in-law of Simon? I wish I'd met this Jesus long ago." Thomas heaved a sigh. "I'll go and talk with him, Andrew. I've been hearing others talk of him. There has been so much work lately I've had no chance to hear him speak. Whether I can be a follower of his I do not know, even if he should want me. I'm not sure he's all you think he is, but I'd like to meet and talk with him." The arrangements were made for a future meeting, and Andrew hurried off while Thomas watched him from the doorway before turning back to his work in the carpenter's shop.

"Andrew tells me you are a carpenter, Thomas. Did he mention to you I learned the carpenter's trade in Nazareth? I have always loved the smell of clean new wood. Was your father a carpenter also?" Jesus asked.

"My father worked for a while at learning the carpenter's trade, but it was never in his heart to work with wood. His trade was fishing. He only used the saw and adze when he lost his taste to live longer in Bethsaida. It was my uncle who taught me all I know. It is his shop where I work," answered Thomas.

"A fisherman who lost his taste for Bethsaida and the sea? Your father sounds like no fisherman I've heard of before," exclaimed Jesus.

"I had a brother once. We were twins. He died suddenly of a fever. My father loved us both. We were his greatest pride. People could not tell us apart. Our old home reminded my father too much of his loss. He left the sea and moved to Capernaum. After my brother's death I wanted only to be called Thomas, which means twin. My mother understood my boyish stubbornness. I think my father never did. Perhaps I added to his grief. I do not know. He took sick and died soon after we came to Capernaum. My uncle took us in and looked after my mother and me as his own." Thomas sat down beside Jesus. It was the first time he had mentioned his brother since boyhood. His heart felt lighter than it had in years. He was glad he'd talked about his loss.

"We'll call you Thomas, as you wish," said Jesus. "I understand your feeling for your brother. I do not think it strange you wished to bury your old name after your brother died. You were twins— each part of the other. Did you ever think that it *could* be that way with *all* men, Thomas? All of us are part of each other. The common bond is love. You and Eliel early understood what others often never learn. This is the message which I bring—the love of God for all men everywhere. In learning to love each other we show our love for God. If you learn to love God you learn to love all men. The time will come when you and Eliel will be together again. There can be a time when Eliel and Judah will stand side by side—with God." Jesus placed his hand on Thomas' shoulder. The carpenter from Capernaum looked at Jesus and the tears stood in his eyes.

"Master, can this really be? I have not truly loved God these many years. In my heart there has always been the feeling of resentment because my brother was taken from me. My mother tried to console me. She said it was God's will. I've done my work as honestly as any man. I have lived by the law, but always in my heart a certain anger smoldered there. Lord, I see what Andrew said is true. You *are* the chosen one! I put my trust in you. May I be of your company?"

"You will be one of the twelve, Thomas. I have need of you," said Jesus. He called the other disciples to him and told them to greet their newest brother, Thomas.

125

Let Us Die with Him

The disciples were gathered in a place not far from Jerusalem. They had journeyed through much of Israel these past thirty months or so. Their travels had taken them as far north as the foothills of Mount Hermon and south to the desert of Judea. The most dangerous journey of all lay just ahead. As the disciples gathered around Jesus and he talked to them, a messenger came seeking Jesus.

"Master, I bring you news from Martha and Mary, sisters of Lazarus. Their brother is very ill. Unless you come to them they fear he will die. They beg you to come to Bethany and attend their brother Lazarus."

Jesus listened to the messenger and sent him back to Bethany with word that he would come soon. For two days Jesus talked with the disciples and instructed them. Then he said, "Come, let us go to Lazarus."

Some of the disciples protested, saying it was too dangerous. Others reminded Jesus that twice already he had been subjected to stoning and had been fortunate to escape with his life.

"Our friend Lazarus is asleep. I go to wake him from his sleep," Jesus told the disciples.

"If he sleeps then it is well," said one of the disciples, not understanding what Jesus was saying.

Jesus spoke more plainly. "Lazarus is dead. Let us go to him."

There were murmurs of protest and an uneasy shifting of feet. Not one disciple stood up and prepared to go with Jesus. Then Thomas stood up and spoke. "Let us go, that we may die with him," he said. Slowly the others began to prepare to go with Jesus. Thomas was not a leader. He seldom spoke out at all. Now he had made his decision and he was prepared to follow it. Whatever the others did, Thomas was going to follow Jesus. Thomas made the others ashamed of their own hesitation. Each one hurried to be in the front rank with Jesus. Thomas walked at his slow, steady pace as the others hurried by him down the road toward Bethany.

"Lord, had you been here my brother would not have died." Martha came running out to greet Jesus as he came down the road to the house of Lazarus. Standing nearby with the other disciples, Thomas could only shake his head in silent sympathy. Then he heard the words Jesus spoke, and the old pain came into his heart.

"Your brother shall rise again," Jesus said to Martha. *Martha's* brother will rise again—but not Eliel. A sadness came over Thomas. Later, when Lazarus was restored to life, Thomas tried to join in the happiness around him, but it was hard.

The days moved on, and all things happened just as Jesus had told them they would. Like many of the others Thomas had not grasped the real meaning of Jesus' words. That night in Gethsemane, when the soldiers led by Judas took Jesus, almost spelled the end for Thomas. He had believed! He had kept the faith with courage even when he had not understood! Jesus had always been there to keep his faith alive. Now everything was gone.

Unlike some of the others who ran in panic through the night, Thomas was calm. A kind of deathly numbness settled over him. Everything was finished. There was nothing left. He turned his face away from Jerusalem. Only the carpenter shop in Capernaum remained. He'd been a fool to leave. Jesus had promised him that one day Judah and Eliel would stand together again. He had seen Lazarus restored to life, and if that could happen then surely he would see Eliel again. But now Jesus had been taken and put to death. He had not saved himself. What was left now? Thomas began the long walk first to Jericho, then on to Capernaum. It was a dangerous road to travel alone. Thomas did not care. There was nothing any robber could take from him now. He had nothing

127

left to lose. The night was cool. He walked until he grew tired and rested by the roadside wrapped in his cloak.

At the first village he begged his breakfast. "Have you any work a carpenter can do? I have no tools, but I can work anything in wood you might need if you have a few tools I can use." At first the man seemed doubtful of Thomas' skill. At last he gave him a broken plow beam to repair, handing him an ax and a knife. It was hard work, but Thomas worked away until at last the plow beam was repaired. There was a chest the farmer's wife had treasured and which would not close properly. Thomas was able to fix the broken lid.

The farmer was so pleased he asked Thomas to stay with him. He and his neighbors would help him to set up a shop. They needed a carpenter. Thomas shook his head and took only a small parcel of food and a water jug. Soon he was on his way. It was late afternoon now. The sun burned hot on the dusty road to Jericho. Thomas did not mind the sun. He had no thought for anything except to get away from all that had betrayed him. Now the only place he cared to be was back in his uncle's carpenter shop in Capernaum. There he could work with his hands and shut his mind to all else. This was work he understood. You measured carefully, chose the right wood, and followed the pattern. When you were finished you knew what you had. There were no riddles to being a carpenter.

He walked steadily, resting when he grew tired, and walked again. At last he came to Jericho. The greenery of the city was soothing after the barren limestone hills. He sat by a well and filled his earthen jug. He spent more time resting than he had intended. At last he got to his feet and started on his way out of the city. Turning the corner of the street he almost fell over a boy huddled against a building. The boy was only a bundle of rags and he was crying bitterly.

"What's the matter, lad?" asked Thomas. The boy looked up at him. He might have been ten, perhaps even twelve. It was hard to tell. He was small, but the face was older than a child's. The boy stopped crying.

"I'm lame. I cannot walk without my crutch. I fell and broke it, so now I cannot walk." The boy held out the broken pieces of a rude crutch for Thomas to see. Thomas looked at the crutch. It hadn't been much to begin with. Certainly there was no way to repair it. He knelt and bent over the boy.

"Do you know where there is a carpenter's shop?" he asked.

"Oh, yes," the boy replied. "The shop of Nahum the carpenter is not far away, but I have no money to pay Nahum to make a new crutch for me."

"Put your arms around my neck and hold on. Hurry now. I've spent too much time here already." Thomas' voice was gruff, but the small boy wasted no time in putting his arms around Thomas' neck and clinging to the disciple's back. Following the boy's directions, Thomas quickly found Nahum's shop. Nahum was busy but he was not an unkind man. When Thomas explained his need of a few scraps of wood and the loan of some tools, Nahum scratched his head. The scraps of wood were no problem, but he did not like his precious tools in untrained hands. At last Thomas convinced him he would not damage them.

Quickly Thomas went to work. From a piece of straight board left over from the top of a chest he sawed a length, carefully measuring the length under the lame boy's arm. Using only a saw, draw knife, and sanding stone he fashioned a smooth, sturdy upright. Now he cut a smaller piece for the arm rest. With chisel, mallet, and slender knife he cut away the wood, leaving two slender pegs extending from the upright. Carefully he measured the arm rest and with the slender knife cut two holes. Turning the thin blade of the knife with endless patience Thomas gradually deepened the holes. At last they fit snugly over the pegs of the upright. Watching Thomas' patient work, Nahum brought him the glue pot.

129

The arm rest was glued securely to the upright. With knife and sanding stone Thomas made a gentle curve and polished the wood so smoothly the lame boy's eyes shone like stars as he watched.

At last Thomas was finished. He handed the crutch to the delighted boy. With his new crutch under his arm the agile little fellow almost danced about the shop. He stammered his thanks and was gone out the door and down the street. Carefully Thomas wiped the tools he had used and put each back in place.

Nahum watched with careful eyes. He had never seen a carpenter work so quickly or more skillfully. "You are a good carpenter, friend. Why are you not working at your trade?" asked Nahum. "There's work for you here if you want to stay. I could use help here in my shop."

Thomas shook his head. "I left a carpenter shop in Capernaum to follow a dream. I am returning to Capernaum." He turned back from the bench and went away from the shop, waving good-bye to Nahum. Ahead of him he saw the lame boy still dancing on his one crutch in the street. He was as active as any boy could be. Thomas didn't smile often, but at the sight of the happy boy he smiled. This lame boy is walking and *I* made him walk. Not the way Jesus could have done, but in the only way I can.

He turned and walked away. Suddenly he stopped. He wasn't going to Capernaum! He was going back to Jerusalem! He had been following no dream. It had been a reality—as real as the crutch he had just made with his own hands. Jesus was gone, but the lessons he had taught them all were still there. "If you learn to love God and love all men"—the words came back to Thomas. It would never be the same. Jesus was gone, but the work he had begun was still there. There were still his teachings to be passed on. Perhaps he and Eliel would never meet again, but there were other boys who needed help. Thomas started back toward Jerusalem. The lame boy waved to him as he passed by. Thomas smiled again. Jesus was gone, but Thomas was still here. I would gladly have died for him, thought Thomas to himself. Surely I can learn to live for him. He began to walk more quickly.

Unless I See for Myself

Andrew had been especially worried about Thomas. He knew his own doubts and weaknesses and he could understand how Thomas must feel. The other disciples had gradually gathered together, but Thomas was still missing. When the door opened and Thomas walked in, Andrew was the first to greet him.

"Thomas, we have seen the Lord! He has risen from the tomb. We have seen him!" The happiness in Andrew's voice as he greeted his friend brought a frown to Thomas' face. He had been prepared for most things, but not for this. He shook his head.

"I'll never believe that, Andrew, until I see for myself. I had a hard time understanding all that Jesus taught us when he was here with us. When I knew he was gone, I wanted only to leave Jerusalem. Then at last I came to realize I was running away from my own sorrow and disappointment. I know things will never be the same, but I'm back to do what I can. I made a lame boy walk." He stopped as Andrew's eyes widened in surprise. "Oh, no, not the way Jesus made the lame walk. I made a crutch for a boy who needed one. It made me realize there are things I can do. I'm here to do what I can do."

Andrew put his arm around Thomas. "I worried about you. I'm glad you're here again. You'll see, Thomas. Someday you'll see with your own eyes what the rest of us saw. You'll see."

131

Now that the eleven disciples were together, they spent the days talking and planning. Carefully they went over everything Jesus had told them, everything he had taught them. Day by day their spirit and convictions grew stronger. Thomas was still his usual quiet self. He talked little, but he listened to all that was said.

As usual, the disciples were together for the evening meal. It was some eight days after Jesus had appeared to all of them except Thomas.

"Peace be unto you." Thomas turned around as he heard the familiar voice he had never expected to hear again. He looked up and Jesus was standing there.

"Thomas, look at my hands. Touch my side. Believe that I am here."

"My Lord and my God!" Thomas could say no more. His heart was pounding. There was a feeling of such happiness and joy within him he felt his chest would burst. Even as he watched, Jesus disappeared. For the first time in all the time he had known Jesus, Thomas really understood. Jesus would always be with them. They would not walk the dusty roads together in Judea, Galilee, and Samaria, but still Jesus would be with them. No matter where Thomas went, Jesus would be there. He thought of all the tears he'd shed in Eliel's name. Why, they had been shed for his *own* loneliness! His own loneliness! With Jesus there had been no loneliness. He, Thomas, had made a lame boy dance for joy just through a certain skill in working wood. No! There had been more to it than that. There had been compassion reaching out to another's need. That was one of the things Jesus had taught them.

Solemn Thomas smiled. Without his being aware, Jesus must have been with him as he shaped the wood for the crutch. All of these past many months when he worked with Jesus, Thomas had been living in a whole new world. Now he could really see it.

132

Let others grieve. Jesus lived! Thomas had seen him, had talked with him. There had been too many years wasted in grief. For the rest of his life Thomas would do the Master's work joyfully. He turned back to the table and saw Andrew looking at him and smiling.

MATTHEW
Who Found a New Way

The caravan from Damascus came to a halt. It was a small caravan. Not more than twelve camels began to slowly kneel at the command of the leader of the caravan. The *mokhes* came out from his booth to examine the goods bound for the market in Capernaum. His assistant, with the help of the camel drivers, began to examine the goods. The *mokhes,* who was the tax collector on goods to be offered in the Capernaum market, began to make his tally. Carefully he marked down the exact count in each camel's load, noting the quantity and type of merchandise. The day was hot. The camel drivers had thrown aside their cloaks and even removed their headdresses as they helped open the woven baskets of goods securely tied to each camel. Only the caravan master kept his cloak wrapped closely about him as he leaned against the tax collector's booth, taking advantage of the shade it offered. *Mokhes, gabbai,* publican, tax collector—there were many names for those who levied the Roman tax on merchandise, foodstuff, land, and income.

At last the tax collector's tally was done. He went inside his booth to compute the tax due. He was almost finished, but not quite. In a few minutes he stepped out of his booth again and called to the caravan master.

"The day is hot. Perhaps you'd like a cool drink of water?" Smiling in surprise the caravan master stepped forward and grasped the water jug in both his hands. He drank deeply and handed the jug back to the tax collector.

"Now if you'll throw off your cloak for a moment, you'll be even more refreshed." The publican spoke in an even tone, but there was no mistaking he meant for the cloak to be removed. The caravan master flushed. Sullenly he unbuckled the leather belt at his waist and removed the cloak. A number of lengths of brilliantly dyed silks were secured to the inside of the cloak. The tax collector calmly removed each of the lengths of silk and placed them in a neat pile on the table in front of him. Then he went back to his figures.

The caravan master groaned and dropped his head. Only too well he knew what was coming next. Smuggled, or undeclared, goods were forfeit. With the price of silk as high as it was, the profits of the small caravan lay on the tax collector's table. How could he face his partner, Jemuel! He'd have to sell some of the camels to get back to Damascus. They were ruined!

The tax collector looked up from his work. He had calculated the tax due. He showed the papyrus on which his tally was figured to the downcast caravan master. Aran, the caravan master and half owner of the caravan, looked at the tally and the tax due. His eyes widened. It could not be true! He looked up at the *mokhes*.

135

"This is my tax? This is all you ask?"

"Matthias, the silk merchant, will pay you a good price for your silks. I understand why you hesitated to place them in your camel baskets. If robbers had attacked you on the way, the silk might have escaped unnoticed hidden under your cloak, but not with a tax collector, Aran. I collect only the tax that is due. Others may have other ways. Make sure you show *all* your goods when you come this way again." He handed the pile of silks back to Aran.

The confused caravan master stuttered his thanks and quickly counted out the tax money from his purse. With a great waving of hands he got his caravan started again. Aran had run into many tax collectors in his time, but this was the first one who took no more than was justly due and passed up the opportunity to confiscate goods worth a year's wages. The next time he came to Capernaum he'd make sure this was the *mokhes* to whom he paid his tax. He still could hardly believe his good fortune. The tax collector had the power to take all his silk for himself. At the very least Aran had expected to lose two-thirds of the silk.

Levi, the tax collector, smiled. He was a small man, but he held himself so straight he often seemed taller than he really was. From the open door of his booth he saw a familiar figure coming up from the shore. A man leading two heavily laden donkeys came up the road. Now the grumbling will soon start, thought Levi to himself. Zebedee with his catch of fish bound for the market would have his usual complaints for Levi.

"Well, here I am, O mighty arm of Herod! Make your tally and steal the goods of honest men to line your own pockets with silver. Too bad *you* don't have to work for your living. It's sad to see a Galilean with his hand in the pockets of his fellow Galileans!" Zebedee continued with his grumbling as Levi and his assistant looked at the fish and estimated the weight and the value.

"No *mousht* in the catch this time, Zebedee?" asked Levi.

"Hah, if you were a fisherman you'd know this isn't the best month for *mousht*. Common fish is the best my men can bring in these days. See that your count is accurate. I'll not be cheated, you know," replied Zebedee.

"You're right about that. You'll not be cheated by me. You'll pay just what the tax should be and not a shekel more, or less either for that matter," said Levi, handing his tally sheet to Zebedee.

"H-mm, well, I'll say that you're fairer than the *gabbai* who collects the land income tax. And that's not saying anything to make you too proud of yourself. Herklon, may his teeth fall out and his stomach shrivel, squeezes us all until we've nothing left. Soon I'll have no business at all to tax. My two sons have gone wandering off after this rabbi from Nazareth they think is so wonderful. Simon and Andrew have deserted me as well! I'm too old to go back in the boats myself. Soon there'll be nothing left of the business." Still grumbling and shaking his head, Zebedee counted out three denarii to pay his fish tax and prodded the two donkeys toward the marketplace.

It was a slow day. There was little commerce coming into Capernaum. Levi began to think about Zebedee's words. The rabbi from Nazareth had spoken in the synagogue just the past sabbath. Levi wasn't especially welcomed there, but he was a Jew and he attended the synagogue services. Of course he had never been one of the seven chosen to recite the *Shema,* or read the Law, or even recite the closing prayer. He never would receive such an honor. There was no chance of anything like that for Levi, the publican. For the most part his fellow Jews hurried by him without speaking.

Levi had *some* friends, of course. There were other tax collectors and minor officials in Capernaum who welcomed his friendship. At home there was only his old grandfather, Jerah, since the death of his father and mother. It was a lonesome life being a Jewish tax collector in Capernaum. Levi lived well enough, for the job paid well even without cheating. His father and his grand-father had both been tax collectors. When Jerah had grown too old for the job, Levi's father had taken over. At fourteen Levi began helping his father, and on his father's sudden death he had taken over as *mokhes*.

Even as a boy Levi had had few friends. The son of a tax collector could never be a very popular boy in a synagogue school. Levi had never married. It seemed unlikely he would. Not that there weren't plenty of girls who'd like to live in a house like Levi's. But there was a certain girl who had caught Levi's eye. Once or twice he thought she had returned his look, but he couldn't be sure. He had never spoken to her. The problem was that her father was Seth, the ruler of the synagogue. No daughter of Seth's would ever be permitted to marry a tax collector. Levi sighed, thinking about it. He'd dreamed some dreams, but he knew they had little chance of coming true.

His thoughts drifted back again to the new rabbi. He wondered if Zebedee's sons and the sons of the fishing fleet owner's partner really had left the fishing fleet to follow the rabbi from Nazareth. Perhaps it was just Zebedee's way of exaggerating in order to have something to grumble about. The young men may have taken a few days off to hear the fellow speak and Zebedee was upset. Maybe Levi himself would go to hear him. He had almost gone to Judea to hear the one called John the Baptizer speak, but Jerah, his grandfather, had protested so much about his leaving his post he hadn't gone. Jacob, Levi's nephew who served as his assistant, was capable enough. He could look after things for a while. This time he wouldn't tell Jerah anything.

"Jacob, I must go away for a while. Perhaps I'll be gone over-night, maybe only for a few hours. I'm not sure. If I am not back tonight, open up at the usual hour in the morning. I'll be here by noon at the latest. Just tell Jerah I've been called away." Levi smiled at the young eighteen-year-old who towered above him. Jacob nodded and came into the booth to take his uncle's place.

Levi hurried toward the marketplace. He knew where to get information about the rabbi from Nazareth. Elias the scribe knew everything that went on in Capernaum and beyond—far beyond, some said. They whispered behind their hands when they mentioned Elias' name. It was rumored the scribe had powerful connections in Jerusalem. Levi soon found Elias' place of business. It was on the corner of one of the busiest streets in the marketplace. Elias' tent was square and the front was open. The floor was covered with rugs, and cushions were scattered about the floor. In front of a small, low desk sat Elias. Behind him were pots of ink of different colors, quills to write with, papyrus rolls, sheets of papyrus and wax tablets.

Levi was in luck. There were no customers at the moment for the several services Elias offered. The old man would be eager to talk.

"Good morning, Elias. May I talk with you for a moment?" asked Levi. Elias waved his visitor to a cushion near his desk.

"What brings a tax collector away from his booth before the hour of closing?" asked the scribe.

"Elias, have you heard this one called Jesus of Nazareth speak?"

The white-haired old man in front of Levi looked at him sharply before he answered. "Yes, I've heard him speak. First in the synagogue and then again in the hills outside the city just two days ago. They say the people are coming to hear him in increasing numbers. If all the rumors I hear about him are true, he'll bear watching. Of course, you can never believe all you hear. You Galileans are emotional people. Let one little thing stir you up and you make a commotion. I myself am from Jerusalem, as perhaps you know."

"As you say, this is a man who may bear watching. Where do you suppose a person would go to hear him?" Levi asked.

"So the little *mokhes* has big ears! H-mm, you surprise me, Levi. Have you ambitions to become a *gabbai*? I've been told you never take a shekel more than is due. Lucius, the Roman in charge of all the tax collection, says your accounts are the most accurate of all the tax collectors in his district."

"No, Elias, I'm not spying on the man and I have no ambitions to be a *gabbai*. I heard Jesus speak in the synagogue. I think I'd like to hear him again. I thought perhaps you'd know where he might be speaking. Thank you for your time. I'll go ask elsewhere."

"Who in Capernaum has more accurate information than Elias? Nobody! If you want to hear this Jesus fellow, you'll find him in the hills to the north of the city. He usually begins his preaching in the late afternoon, I'm told. There's your information, Levi. You'll find no need to ask anyone else. I still believe you're a *mokhes* with big ears, but of course that's not my affair. A tax collector who leaves his booth just to hear a preacher from the hill country of Galilee? Hah! I'm not a fool, you know!" Elias was still spouting words as Levi hurried from his tent.

There was a fairly large crowd gathered when Levi reached the low hill where Jesus was speaking. He sat down on the ground near the edge of the crowd and listened.

"Ask and it will be given to you. Seek and you will find. Knock and the door shall be opened to you. Everyone who asks, receives. He who seeks, finds what he seeks. What man among you, if his son asks for bread, gives him a stone? Or if he asks for fish, gives him a serpent? If you, as imperfect as you are, give good gifts to your children, how much more shall your Father who is in heaven give good things to those who ask him for them."

There was a great deal more, but these were the words which spoke directly to Levi. He felt as if Jesus were speaking to him alone. The truth was, Levi was not happy. The job of collecting taxes was not a happy way of life for him. It was not that he felt the dishonor others attached to his job. He had preserved his own sense of honor by collecting only the tax which was due. He had cheated neither the authorities over him nor the people from whom he collected the tax. Still, it was a lonely and unsatisfying life. And there was Rhoda, the daughter of Seth. He wished he could forget her. No, that wasn't being honest! What he really wished was that he could go to her father with the hope of arranging a marriage. Levi shook his head as he walked, with the crowd, back to Capernaum. This new teacher was a wonderful speaker. He really made you believe you could start a whole new life. "Knock and the door shall be opened." If it only *could* be opened. Levi walked slowly toward his house, thinking. If only there was a way. He sighed. He had a good life—much to be thankful for. But what was food on the table if you weren't happy? Jerah would never understand how he felt.

At home there were the explanations Jerah demanded. Where had he been? Listening to the Nazarene again? Jerah's remarks were more cutting than usual. When at last he could get away and go to his own room, Levi shut the door and took out his writing materials. He wrote down all he could remember of what Jesus had said. It would be good to have these words to read whenever he wanted them. Perhaps he would always be a tax collector, but these words took his mind away from the tax booth—far away.

Twice more he found a way to take a few hours from his duties and listen to Jesus. He always worked his way to the very front so as not to miss a word of what was said. Fortunately Jerah did not find out. More and more words of the one called Jesus were set down for the tax collector to read and re-read. Weeks went by, and it was no longer possible for Levi to get away. It was the season when the caravans came most frequently. Levi was busy, but he couldn't put the tall teacher out of his mind. Often at night he read over again the words he had put down.

141

One morning a shadow across the window of his booth caused Levi to look up. Here was no merchant. Why, it was the teacher from Nazareth! Quickly Levi came out of his booth. He looked into the face of the taller man.

"Levi, come follow me."

"Me? You want me? You're the teacher from Nazareth! I heard you speak weeks ago."

"I saw you in the crowd, Levi. I want you to work with me in a special kind of way. It won't be easy work. There will be danger and there will be hard days ahead. You'll make new friends and perhaps enemies as well."

"Enemies, Master? A tax collector knows something about having enemies! I'll come with you. My nephew is here with me. There are things I must explain to him so that he can take over my duties. Teacher, will you dine with me this evening? It will be my way of saying farewell to this kind of life, showing my old friends Levi, the tax collector, is no more. I must explain that my grandfather, who lives with me, will not dine with us. He is confined to his bed. He will not be happy with my decision to follow you. Will you come, Master?"

"Of course, Levi. I'll come and bring my friends with me. You'll be the newest of my followers. You spoke of leaving your old life. Perhaps you would like a new name to go with your new life. Would you like to be called Matthew? It means *gift of God*. A good name for a man starting a new life." Jesus smiled down at the smaller man.

"Matthew, a new name for a new life. It's a wonderful name! You'll really come and bring your friends with you tonight?"

"Come later this afternoon and extend your invitation to them yourself. They'll welcome you. You'll see." Jesus turned and walked away, leaving the tax collector staring after him. There would be no turning back for Levi now. All the weeks of indecision were over. He would follow a new life with Jesus of Nazareth.

The Scroll

The supper was almost over. All of Levi's friends had come. Tax collectors, various officials of the government, some merchants who made it their business to be friendly to all tax collectors—even Lucius in charge of all tax collections in Galilee was there. Never had any of them seen a more lavish supper prepared. Roasted bullock, lamb, birds, fish, pastries, and fruits were served. The best wines had been brought out. The strangest thing about the whole affair was that the guest of honor seemed to be the teacher from Nazareth who was becoming talked about in Capernaum these days. And with him were the sons of Zebedee, the owner of the largest fishing fleet in Capernaum. Simon-bar-Jonah and his brother Andrew were there as well. Lucius wondered about these people. He didn't understand why they were there. Levi had always been one of his steadiest men. He hoped no trouble was brewing.

Levi called for the attention of his guests. He stood up before them as they turned toward him. "The hour is late. I appreciate the honor you all have done me in dining with me this evening. Now I have something to tell you. Levi the tax collector is through collecting taxes! From now on I am a follower of Jesus of Nazareth." Levi pointed toward Jesus where he stood with his small group of disciples around him.

"There is something more you should know. I have taken a new name to go with my new way of life. Henceforth I will be known as Matthew. Levi the tax collector is no more! From now on it will be Matthew, the follower of Jesus of Nazareth!" Levi—or Matthew as he would be called from now on—stepped back as his guests gathered around him. Lucius pushed forward through the crowd.

"You're *really* giving up your post, Levi?" he asked.

Matthew nodded his head in answer.

"You're a strange man, Levi. How can you give up all this to follow a traveling preacher? Today the crowds follow him. Tomorrow perhaps no one will remember his name. If they do remember it, that may be all the worse for him. Mark my words, this John the Baptizer fellow is getting too well known for his own good. *He'll* be in trouble before long. It could happen to your friend Jesus as well. I suppose Jacob will be taking over your post? Well, he seems like a sensible lad. You've taught him well. Goodbye, Levi. I think you're foolish but I wish you well." The bulky Roman walked away without waiting for any reply.

Matthew looked around for Jesus and his friends, but they had already slipped away. As quickly as he could he said good-bye to his remaining guests. He was anxious to start on his new life now that he had made the break with the old. But first there was his grandfather to face again. He had great affection for the old man. He did not want to hurt him, but this was a step he had to take. Tomorrow would be a new beginning. As he returned from saying goodnight to the last guest, the tax collector looked around the large room so recently filled with people. Lucius would never understand how he felt. Matthew wasn't giving up anything; he was gaining a whole new world. He felt happier than he had ever felt before. Matthew hurried to his grandfather's room.

"Why do you do this foolish thing? I followed the profession of tax collector and no man could complain I took more than the tax allowed! Your father manned his post at the Damascus-Acre road after me. No man has just complaint against us. Only the lawful tax has been collected. I have taught strict adherence to the law— no more, no less. If there are tax collectors who cheat, so there are winemakers who water their wine. Is one way of earning an honest living less honorable than another? Isn't it better for the law to be in the hands of honest men than thieves?" Jerah was propped up in his bed. He was old, but his speech was clear and his mind was as keen as any younger man's.

"I have followed your teachings and those of my father always, Jerah. I have never taken more than the tax which was due from any man. It is not a question of honor. I am simply not happy in this work. I do not feel I can ever be truly happy collecting taxes on the goods which come into Capernaum. I have a chance to work with the teacher, Jesus. Some believe he is the Messias, the chosen one of Israel. I do not know. I only know I want to be one of his disciples and to work with him. I feel I must go." Matthew raised his head and looked into the old man's piercing eyes.

"Then go, Levi. No, I'll not call you Matthew. I'm too old for new names and new ways. There is more than enough here to take care of my few needs. Jacob will look after me. Go and find happiness, if you can, Levi. Happiness is not an easy bird to snare. Do you still write down things you want to remember, grandson? If you find your happiness, write down how you found it. Perhaps other men will read it and find theirs through the words you write." Jerah held out his arms to his grandson, and for a moment the stern hawk-face became gentle. A few minutes later Levi-Matthew tiptoed from the room. Already his grandfather was sleeping.

The thinning white hair and the wispy white beard betrayed his age. The short, trim figure and the quick, unhesitant step gave the impression of a younger man. The impression was heightened by the clear brown eyes as alert as a youth's. And yet there was no denying the fact the man who sat at the small writing desk had lived a long and full life. Even now he was trying to recall that life. It wasn't an account of his own life he was writing—though he had been there for part of the record he was trying to set down. The scroll he was writing would be an account of all he could recall from what he knew, from what he had been told, and from what he had read of the story of Jesus and what Jesus had taught.

For many years he had thought about writing down all he knew.

145

He raised his eyes and looked through the window in the wall to his left. It was late afternoon but the sun was still in the sky. It had been such an afternoon with the sun in the sky when he had climbed the mountain with the multitude who followed Jesus. It was that day when he had heard the wonderful words of the sermon Jesus had preached on the mountainside. At that time he had said to himself, this should be written down. These words must be saved for others to read. Some of them he *had* written down. "Blessed are they that mourn: for they shall be comforted." These and other parts of that sermon he had memorized. Many times he had said them over to himself.

That was the first time he had thought of writing it all down. Later, as he had the opportunity to work with Jesus and others of the twelve, he had thought again, someday I must write all this down. But there had been so much to learn and the days had flown so quickly. It seemed there was never any time to write. Then had come the Passover journey to Jerusalem. Remembering after all these years, the pain came into his heart again. How blind they had been! Time and again Jesus had tried to prepare them. But when the blow finally came and Jesus was taken from them, the sudden realization of his warnings had come too late.

The old man got up from his chair. He walked to the window. He was not tall enough to see the ground through the window but he could look up at the sky. It was an old habit. He'd always looked upward. Now it was growing darker. Just as it had grown dark in Gethsemane on that evening long ago. He had slept! While Jesus prayed, he had slept! Only when the soldiers came to take his Master had he awakened. He had awakened quickly then, and he had fled! The memory of that time was something all the years between could not erase, nor could the years make the memory less bitter. Remembering, the old man shook his head and sighed.

During that time there had been no thought of writing anything down. There had been only terror and fear. After the trial and the

146

crucifixion, slowly the disciples had come back to gather together again—all except the one who had betrayed him. Then came the good news that Jesus had arisen! Peter and John had seen the empty tomb! And then Jesus had come to them again. Yes, it had to be written down—all of it. John Mark had written much of it, but there were things to be added. Things he knew because he had been there when they happened. He himself had not so many years left. The years of laboring in Parthia had taken their toll of him. If the scroll he had always wanted to write was to be written, it must be now. When he had finished it he would go back to Parthia, to Ethiopia—wherever there were those who wanted to hear the good news, he would go. There were only a few of them left now. Once there had been twelve. But first he would write down what he knew. Not his own life, but the writing which would tell about Jesus and his work.

The old man walked back to his desk and sat down again. He drew the parchment toward him and took up his pen. He turned in annoyance at the footsteps behind him. He wanted to be alone.

"Matthew, I've brought a lamp. The light is growing dim. If you must sit here and write, you'll need a lamp." The man who brought the lamp was almost as old as Matthew himself. Smiling now, the man at the desk took the lamp from the hands of his friend. "Thank you, Thaddaeus. The light is welcome."

Now the one called Matthew began to write. Slowly his pen formed the words of the beginning: "The book of the generation of Jesus Christ . . ." He stopped, and for an instant he remembered the words of another very old man, spoken to him many years before.

"If you find your happiness, write down how you found it. Perhaps other men will read it and find theirs through the words you write." As Jerah's words came back to him, Matthew smiled and picked up his pen again. These would be the words which would tell how he had found his happiness—how all men could find their happiness.

147

SIMON ZELOTES
The Gentle Warrior

There was a crescent moon high in the sky and slim as the curved blade of a *sica*. Now and then wisps of cloud trailed across the moon. The darkness these moments brought was welcomed by the band of men moving carefully along the dry bed of Wadi el Ames. It was a small band. There were only six, moving in single file, each no more than an arm's length from the one nearest him.

Barabbas was the leader. Small, well put together, and wiry, with skin burned brown as dry oak leaves, the leader of the band moved noiselessly even in the dark. Simon, his second-in-command, was a giant of a man. He towered over his leader and all the others of the small group. Despite his size he moved as catlike as Barabbas.

Joel, Jether, Micah, and Laban completed the roster. All except Laban were young men in their mid-twenties. No one knew the age of Laban. His hair was snow white. He kept it cut short and wore no beard. He was strong and lithe and lean. Laban was no longer young, but none dared call him old. The curved blade at his side had tasted Roman blood many times. No one swung his *sica* with deadlier effect than Laban.

These were men who had sworn the Zealot's oath. Their aim: to free this land of Roman rule. They came from all over Palestine. Their backgrounds were as different as the towns and villages from whence they came. Barabbas, the leader of the group, was the son of a rabbi in Jerusalem. Simon's father had been a maker of shoes and sandals in Cana. Joel was from Tarichaea and had worked in the fish-drying plant there. Jether came from Jericho. Micah had been a fisherman and called Hammath his home. Laban was Galilean. He volunteered no information as to where his home had been or how he had lived before. He was skillful in all things. He could sew with needle and thread, build a snare to catch a bird, work at the blacksmith's forge, and was better than most with the carpenter's tools. But above all, he excelled at killing Romans.

The chain which linked these men together was skill, strength, determination, cunning, and hate. When everything was said, hate was the strongest link in the chain. Each of them hated Romans. Some for one reason, some for another. Whatever the reasons for their hate the common cause bound them together. There were some who regarded them as heroes, patriots fighting to free their land from a tyrant's rule. And there were those who called them murderers and thieves. There were others who neither condemned nor applauded them, but simply regarded Zealots as fools with no chance for success.

This was a raiding party. Their goal, a Roman camp below Arbel in Galilee. Silently they picked their way along the rocky, dry creek bottom of the wadi. In the time of rains, where they walked could be a raging torrent. Now it was bone dry. The wadi roughly paralleled the road. Barabbas had word a small detachment of Roman soldiers were left in the camp while the main body had gone north to Capernaum. They were to meet a high Roman official coming from Damascus. The soldiers would be his escort to Jerusalem.

Six silent men with short swords swinging in the dark could take on ten better-armed Roman soldiers and hope to win—if the Romans were taken by surprise. But surprise was the Zealots' only advantage. Unless surprised, the ten Romans would make short work of even such hardened fighters as these men. Barabbas reached back and touched Simon on the shoulder. Immediately the signal was passed down the line. Silently they halted. Up ahead the wadi turned and, following the turn, widened so the sides became shallow and provided much less cover. The camp was near. It was time to pause and make sure each man knew the plan.

They gathered around their leader, and Barabbas went over each detail in low tones. He tapped Laban on the shoulder. The older man went on ahead. The others waited. In a few minutes he was back. The way ahead was clear. They resumed their single file as before. Once more Laban dropped to the rear. A few yards past the turn Barabbas led them up out of the wadi and along the road. The wadi no longer afforded cover. They could move faster on the road with no greater risk. The clouds no longer befriended them. The slice of moon was clear as silver in the sky. Again the leader passed the silent signal back and the band halted, each man flattening himself along the road. Barabbas pointed. Ahead and to the left the outline of a tent appeared. The camp was sixty yards away.

When the small group moved forward this time, the line of march had changed. Now Simon led and, at his right shoulder,

150

Laban was half a step behind—no more. Barabbas and Micah trotted together five yards back. Five yards back of them Joel and Jether moved side by side. Simon had thrown off his cloak. A dagger swung in his belt at his left side, the short curved *sica* at his right. Laban at his shoulder kept his *sica* sheathed, but his dagger was in his right hand. The four others carried their daggers in their left hands and the short, curved swords in their right.

Stumps of hacked-down trees bordered the camp. They had been chopped down to make sure the view of the road was not blocked. These had been fig trees bearing fruit for fifty years. Now they were rotting stumps. The pace slowed to a careful walk. Now only Simon and Laban moved slowly forward. The other four hugged the slim shadows by the roadside. A solitary soldier walked his post. The faint moon reflected off the brass helmet. Sword in hand, with breastplate girded on, the sentinel patrolled his post.

The sentry had just pivoted to make his slow return march when a giant arm from behind him grasped his throat. The muscles in the soldier's sword arm tightened. He fought for air. Upper arm and forearm closed a deadly vise about his throat. The soldier slumped backward. Simon caught the sword before it fell. He eased the soldier to the ground. Calmly Laban cut the straps on either side which bound the breastplate and backpiece together at the waist. The soldier lay on his back. Laban lifted the breastplate and thrust his dagger home. The Roman soldier had walked his last post.

Even as Laban plunged his dagger home, the four flitting shapes moved silently through the camp. It was here the hate in Laban's heart betrayed him. He was so anxious to kill again he stumbled on the body of the dead Roman. His dagger jarred from his hand and struck the metal breastplate of the fallen sentry. Instantly the camp awoke. Barabbas and Micah had found the first tent they entered empty. Joel and Jether had just reached a larger tent

151

near the center of the camp. It was here where there was trouble.

With so small a force left in camp the ten men—except for the one on sentry duty—slept in the large tent in the center. Now with the clang of steel on steel these veterans who slept with weapons at their side awoke in a flash. The startled Romans burst from the tent just as Joel and Jether reached the entrance. The two Zealots were cut down at once. Laban flew to the action. His lust for blood overflowed all his other senses. He caught one soldier on the arm before he too was killed.

Micah and Barabbas had circled behind the Romans. As the soldiers turned to meet this new attack, Simon with his sword struck down the leader of the Roman detachment. Now the odds were seven Romans against three Zealots. Poor odds in any case. But it was dark and it was hard for the Romans to know how many attacked them. Simon's attack confused them for a moment. Micah fell, but Barabbas thrust his dagger home at close range and killed a Roman. The Romans fell back toward their tent. Barabbas slipped into the shadows of the trees behind the camp. Simon joined him there.

Taking advantage of their knowledge of the land and the confusion in the camp, the two got away. They ran steadily for an hour, turning back across country toward Arbel but keeping to the hills. Finally they crossed the main road to Tarichaea and followed the Wadi el Hammam for a way. Then leaving that, they climbed into the hill country above. At last they stopped to rest. They flung themselves on the ground and gasped for breath. When at last they could speak, it was Barabbas who broke the silence.

"What was the noise that alarmed the camp?" he asked. "I saw you silence the sentry just as we'd planned."

"Laban was too eager to make another kill. He stumbled in his haste to get to the others and dropped his dagger on the breastplate of the man on guard. It was so needless. I had choked the man but Laban must be doubly sure. Then, when he saw the rest of you go by, he feared he would be too late to kill again. His hate betrayed him." Simon sat up, and the big man slowly shook his head and one huge fist pounded the ground beside him.

"Four Romans for four of us. Call it an even swap. Considering the odds, I suppose we can be satisfied with the night's work," Barabbas said and lay back on the ground to rest again.

"I loved Micah as my brother. Four of them for four of us! You call it even, do you? I call it something else. I call it nothing more than madness. I'm no scholar. As anyone can see, I have more strength than brains, but I'll play the fool no more! I'm tired of all this killing. For seven years I've fought and killed the Romans where I could. I swore an oath of vengeance for something which happened long ago. Now I can see there is no way my sword can balance up the score. I had a father once. He is no more, and killing Romans will not bring him back. I'm through, Barabbas! I kill no more." Simon stood up, and taking his short, curved sword he broke it across his knee. He flung each piece as far as far as he could throw. Because he knew well the smaller man who sat there on the ground looking up at him, Simon kept the dagger in his belt not far from his hand.

If Barabbas did not like the words he heard, he gave no indication. "No, you're no fool, my friend Simon. But a man can do a foolish thing and regret it soon thereafter. You've learned the killer's trade and mastered it better than most. Not quite as well as Laban, perhaps, for Laban lived only to kill. What does a man do when he forsakes his trade, Simon?" Barabbas smiled his smile which was no smile at all, but more the look a fox gives when he sights a kill.

"Once long ago I helped my father in his shop make shoes and sandals. That's been some time ago, but I've spent more years helping in the shop than learning how to kill. I still remember how to shape leather to the traveler's foot. What I've forgotten

153

I will learn again. One thing I will *not* do is kill again. I'm tired of that!" The big man said the words with such slow sureness even Barabbas knew more talk was of no use.

"Go your way then, Simon. You go your way. I'll go mine. One day the name Barabbas will be shouted all over Palestine. When it is, you may wish to come and see me. Sica or shoemaker's knife, whichever blade you choose, I'll find a place for you. I never knew a stronger man and few who fought as well. I go toward Jerusalem. Farewell, Simon. A fighter suddenly turned gentle has no place with me. I'd choose a thousand Labans if I could find them. Perhaps someday I will." Barabbas turned away, walking fast in the direction of Jerusalem.

Simon watched him. Then he turned his face across the hills toward Capernaum. He looked back after a short time and saw his old companion disappear from sight. Slowly he drew the dagger from his side and threw it as far as he could throw.

A Child of God

Had he stood up, he would have been easily noticed because of his size. Reclining on the ground, leaning on his elbow, he was not so noticeable. He assumed the position purposely. Sitting upright, as many of the others did, he would have blocked the view of those behind him. Even seated, Simon was an impressive figure. This would be the fourth time he had heard the teacher from Nazareth speak. He had followed with the crowd a long way to hear him speak again. Up the mountainside he had trudged with the others. The cripple he had carried on his back up the steepest part sat near him.

Waiting for the speaker to begin, Simon thought about these last two years. What strange years they had been. The tiny house in the poorest part of Capernaum had somehow become a home. Some would not think of it as much of a home, but it was more than he had had for a long time. There were not many who came to his shop to have their sandals repaired, but each week one or two new customers came. Of course, all his customers were the poorest of the poor. Only the very poor had their sandals repaired. It was better to buy new ones. Someday he'd have the money and the tools to stock hides and make new sandals and shoes. Now he used only scraps of leather and the meagerest of tools. For the first time in a long time Simon felt at peace.

Since boyhood his great size and strength had been something of a burden to him. As a boy he had been bigger than other boys. Somehow his size always seemed a challenge to others. There was always someone who wanted to pit his own strength against Simon's. As sometimes is the case, a giant body housed a gentle heart, and Simon turned aside from every test of strength he could until there was no other way to settle things. He grew into manhood and there were always some who wished to test a big man's powers. Simon learned how not to hear many of the taunts tossed at him. But there were those who mistook gentleness for fear. These men soon learned that lessons earned with broken bones are always long remembered. Simon leaned forward. The one called Jesus of Nazareth was beginning to speak.

"Blessed are the poor in spirit: for theirs is the kingdom of heaven.

"Blessed are they that mourn: for they shall be comforted.

"Blessed are the meek: for they shall inherit the earth.

"Blessed are they which do hunger and thirst after righteousness: for they shall be filled.

155

"Blessed are the merciful: for they shall obtain mercy.

"Blessed are the pure in heart: for they shall see God.

"Blessed are the peacemakers: for they shall be called the children of God."

Jesus continued speaking, and every word he spoke went straight to Simon's heart. Everything the teacher said had meaning for Simon. One of the charges which meant most to Simon was where Jesus had said, "Blessed are the peacemakers: for they shall be called the children of God." For seven years of Simon's life he had been anything but a peacemaker. Before he had joined Barabbas he had turned away from fights. Then he had learned to seek them. Simon recalled something else Jesus had said, and it troubled him. Jesus had said, "You have heard that it was said in times of old—you shall not kill; and whoever kills is in danger of the judgment." There was no way for Simon to evade the truth. He *had* killed, not once but many times. He had to speak to the teacher from Nazareth. Somehow he had to speak to him.

Jesus had finished speaking. The hour was late. Many of those who had come from shorter distances were winding their way home down the mountain. Others who had come from farther off prepared to spend the night here in the open. Tomorrow might be too late. Perhaps tomorrow his courage would be gone. Simon knew he must speak to Jesus now.

Jesus had withdrawn from the crowd to an open place on the level summit. Around him were his disciples. There were always many who wished to press close to Jesus, to speak to him, touch him, to ask some special favor. The disciples tried to protect him. Simon-bar-Jonah, James, and John were the inner guard who stayed closest to Jesus always. Others formed an outer shield against those who pressed in. Simon had climbed down the hillside from where he had been sitting and across the low place formed by a small depression. Now he climbed up to where Jesus and the disciples were talking together.

"I must talk with the teacher." The big man spoke to the disciple who came up to meet him. "It is very important. I would not ask to speak with him if it were not so important."

"Many wish to speak with him, my friend. Wait until morning. He will be rested then. He has talked to all of you for such a long time. Now he needs time to rest and be refreshed. Come again in the morning." Andrew smiled as he looked up at the man before him. This fellow was even bigger than Andrew's brother.

"No, it must be now for me. By tomorrow my courage will have left me. This is the fourth time I have heard the Nazarene speak. Each time I've lacked the courage to try to speak to him. I'll only take a few minutes of his time. May I speak to him?" The simple sincerity in Simon's words touched Andrew's heart.

"Wait here," Andrew replied and turned away to consult with his brother.

"Simon," Andrew addressed his brother, "there is one here who says he must see Jesus. As you can see, he is a giant of a man, but I never heard a man speak more gently or more sincerely. Can we not let him speak to the Master for a moment or two?"

Simon looked over his brother's head at the other Simon. "They all have some special need to see Jesus. And yet, I like this fellow's looks. I've seen him in the crowd before. He hangs on every word the Master says. Bring him here and I will speak to Jesus." Simon-bar-Jonah went to where Jesus sat alone.

"Master, a man is here who says it's most important that he speak with you. I do not know his special need. Will you have me bring him to you?" Simon-bar-Jonah knelt by Jesus' side as he asked the question.

"Every man's need is important to me, Simon. Bring our friend at once," Jesus replied.

Now that he was where he had longed to be, Simon did not

157

know how to begin. He stood looking down on Jesus where the teacher from Nazareth was seated apart from his disciples.

"Sire, I am a man of little learning and I am troubled, for I have committed many transgressions. I know I must be brief and yet I'm not sure how to begin. I . . . I . . ." Simon's voice faltered and he stopped. He had never been much with words and found it difficult to continue.

"Sit down beside me. Do not worry about whether you are brief or not. Begin at the beginning. That's the only place to start a story and I can see you have a story to tell me. What is your name?" The calm, friendly voice of Jesus made the larger man forget his fears. Simon sat down beside Jesus.

"My name is Simon, Master."

"Then sit here beside me, Simon, and tell me all that troubles you."

"I was born in Cana of Galilee, not many miles away. My father had a small shop there. He made sandals and shoes for a living. He had a small plot of land and much of our food came from the garden. I was my father's only child. My mother died in giving birth to me. I only knew my father. He was all that any father could be to a son. I loved him and respected him. Even as a boy I had trouble because of my great size. I was much bigger and stronger than other boys my age. Often there were others older than myself who wished to test my strength. I never liked to fight. While other boys wrestled with each other just to see which of them might win, I never did. I feared I'd hurt one of my friends. Sometimes it happened I could not avoid a fight. When this was so, I won.

"I grew to be a man and at eighteen I could lift a young bullock on my shoulders. I worked with my father and he taught me his craft of working leather, stitching it to shoe the people of our town and any travelers who might need his skill. I was content. As I grew stronger in the first burst of manhood, my father grew more frail and his fingers became stiffer and slower in their work. Still his skill was such that people came from beyond Cana to have their sandals made.

"A group of Roman soldiers stopped in Cana. It was a small detachment of a few men. They did not say why they came. Later I learned they were seeking the leader of a Zealot band. One of the soldiers had a boot he wished to have repaired. He brought it to my father late in the day. Long after we had gone to bed that night there came a knocking at our door. My father lit the lamp and unbarred the door. It was the Roman soldier, drunk with too much wine, demanding his boot. My father told him to come back the next day. He would have the boot repaired before noon. The soldier cursed my father for his slowness and in his drunken rage swung and knocked my father down. I came into the room just in time to see the blow that struck my father. He was an old man. The blow which struck him caused his head to hit the corner of his work table. When I picked him up I could see that he was dead.

"The soldier drew back, startled at what he had done. He was sober now. But it was late for sober thoughts for him. I reached him in a bound. These two hands I hold before you choked out his life in less time than the telling takes. And so it all began. I had taken my first life." Simon paused and looked down at his hands, clasping and unclasping them.

"But there is more that you would tell me, Simon," Jesus said.

"Aye, Master, there is more, much more," Simon replied and began again.

"Whatever justification a man might have for slaying the killer of his father I surely had. But I had taken Roman life and I knew mine was forfeit. I took a few belongings and I fled. Into the hills I fled. I'd walked every mile of them. From Cana to Capernaum there was no path I did not know or fox's hole I could not find.

"There in those hills I met a man who led a band of men who hated Romans as did I. So I joined them. I cannot speak the leader's name. We walked together seven years before we parted. I would not betray him now, though his way and mine were never the same. They called themselves Zealots. Their oath was to rid our land of Roman rule. Some of them felt theirs was a holy war. I was neither patriot nor spurred by holy zeal. I hated all Roman soldiers because one had killed my father.

"Under the guidance of our leader we raided when and where we could. Many of our number were killed and we killed many Romans in return. At last there came a time when I began to weary of the game we played. My hate had burned itself to embers. And then we made a raid. Just six of us—the best fighters of us all. We were the best because we'd been at it longer than the rest. Only the skillful ones survive for long. We made a raid on a Roman camp. Our six against their ten. One of our men made a mistake which cost us dearly. We left four Romans dead and two of us got away. Our leader and I fought free and fled.

"I decided I'd had enough of killing. I broke my sword and threw away my dagger. Now I mend sandals for a living. This is my story, Master, but there is still more. Perhaps you'll not believe me, and yet it's true. I am a peaceful man. You said these hours ago, 'Blessed are the peacemakers: for they shall be called the children of God.' I would be a child of God! And yet I have killed, and for the killing I have done I am in danger of judgment. How can a man in danger of judgment for such as I have done become a child of God?" The big man had finished his story and asked his question.

"Simon, you have carried a heavy burden for a long time, but already you've begun to lighten your load. You are truly sorry for the lives which you have taken. That is the first step. Even before you threw down your sword you were weary of it. Then you threw down your sword and took up other ways. This was

160

the second step. Now you wish to walk in ways of peace and become a child of God. Your Father in heaven hears every prayer. Whatever we have been need not keep us from becoming better. I need a man who wants to be a child of God. Will you work with me, Simon? You'll never have to use a sword, but there will be times when the sword may be used against you. Can you face that and not strike back?" Jesus looked into Simon's face.

"Master, if you will let me work for you, knowing all you know of me, I will never raise my hand in anger against any man no matter whose hand is raised against me." Simon's dark eyes burned with an eagerness they'd never had before.

Jesus stood up and Simon stood beside him. A few yards away the other disciples sat around a small fire kindled for the evening meal. "Come, Simon, I'll call you Simon Zelotes, Simon the Zealot, to distinguish you from my other Simon. Now your zeal will be for God and, loving God, all men as well." Jesus took his newest disciple by the hand and walked with him to the others.

"Here is your newest brother," Jesus said, "Simon Zelotes is one of us." Each one in turn put his arms around the new disciple. Matthew laughed when his turn came. "A tax collector with his arms around a Zealot! And such arms as yours, Simon! I'm glad you're one of us and I'm not collecting Roman taxes anymore."

The Peacemaker

On the edge of the crowd a giant of a man stood watching. He was tall enough to see over the heads of those who stood in front

161

of him. Slowly Simon Zelotes edged through the crowd. Grudgingly people gave way, and the man stopped in the center of the crowd, not far from where Pilate stood with Jesus before him and the elders of the Sanhedrin pressing around. As was the custom for this feast day Pilate asked the crowd which prisoner they would have him release. He hoped the crowd would speak out for Jesus because he knew it was the jealousy of the high priest alone which had brought Jesus to trial.

As he looked around him, the tall man could see the agents of the Sandedrin whispering into the ears of people in the crowd. Occasionally the clink of silver sounded as coins slipped from one hand to another.

"Barabbas! Barabbas! Release Barabbas!" shouted first one and then another in different sections of the crowd. Gradually the chant became louder.

Pilate beckoned one of his soldiers. The man hurried away. In a few minutes he came back leading a small, wiry man bound in chains. For an instant the man in chains looked into the center of the crowd. The tall man looked at the prisoner. Again the crowd began its chant to free Barabbas. The big man shook his head sadly and turned and slipped back through the crowd.

The forest was dark. Occasional sunlight filtered through the tall oak trees, but the trees were so closely ringed around the open space that even here there was only the strange gray-green light of the forest. The prisoner with his hands tied behind his back was a giant of a man. All his life his size had been the thing which people noticed first. Many marveled at his size and never tried to know the man. That was their loss, for the man was worth the knowing. He was far from home, this man who stood with his hands bound at his back. A forest in Britain was far from the hills of Galilee, but the big man had traveled many places in these last twenty years. Persia, Egypt, North Africa, and now Britain had seen his huge frame and heard his gentle voice tell the good news Jesus had first taught him in Galilee.

"How would you like to live, man from across the seas?" the leader of the forest men asked his prisoner.

Haltingly in this strange tongue he had learned as best he could, Simon Zelotes replied, "If I can live to spread the word of Jesus Christ, my life is worth living."

"Our own gods care for Britons. Whatever strange gods you invoke have no power here, but perhaps there is a way you can save yourself, O man of mighty stature. You count yourself a strong man?"

"Stronger than most, I fear," answered Simon. He was past his middle forties now, and streaks of gray touched his hair and beard, but the mighty muscles bulged as huge as always.

"Good! Then we'll test your strength and skill," replied the other. "Rolf, come out," he cried over his shoulder. In answer to the shout a youth as tall and broad as Simon came from the trees behind the rude bench where the leader sat facing Simon. The man was twenty years younger than Simon and as fair as Simon was dark.

"I'll give each of you a short sword. Nothing else. No shield. We'll see who is the better man. This is your chance to live, dark one. Will you accept the challenge?" The leader was on his feet, eyes sparkling with the thought of the sport to come.

"No," said Simon. "I will not fight."

"Of course you will. You've nothing to lose. If Rolf kills you, as he likely will, you're no more dead than if my sword drops you here and now. If you win I promise freedom. Now say you'll play the game."

"No fighting for me," said Simon. "I broke my sword long ago. I will not pick it up again. I'd rather die than use the sword."

"That's coward's talk," the leader cried. "But if you wish to

163

die a coward's death I'll grant your wish and speed you on your way." He raised his sword, but stepped back as he saw the giant's muscles bulge and snap the ropes which bound his arms.

"Now, let me die a free man," Simon said and, throwing open his tunic, bared his breast to the blade.

The Briton's eyes widened. Quickly the blade plunged home and Simon dropped where he stood. His slayer looked down at him.

"I did not understand his ways but he was brave," the leader of the forest men said. "This Jesus of whom he always talked must be a God of gods to hold a man so fast to him." The forest man shook his head slowly again and walked away.

JAMES-THE-LESS
The Man Who Grew Tall

Most of the land was fertile. Young wheat ripened in the fields. Here in southwest Galilee there was enough rainfall to make the olive trees grow, and groves dotted the hills around Nain. Because most of the land was fertile, the barren pinkish-gray plot of land stood out like a wound amid the gold and green of the fields. It was here the little man dug out the clay to fill the woven baskets slung on either side of his patient donkey.

Digging the clay was hard work, but James was used to hard work. All his life he'd found his small stature made it necessary to be twice the man others were to prove his worth. And so he dug his clay and lifted the heavy earth carefully, balancing the load to ease the burden of his friend as best he could. At

165

last the load was finished and balanced to his satisfaction. Putting the heavy mattock over his own shoulder so as not to add to the donkey's load, the small man led his beast.

He entered the village of Nain and passed down the main street. People smiled and shouted greeting as he passed them. The little man smiled his answer but did not speak. At last he came to a narrow street. It was really little more than a path. He turned down the street and stopped at the last house. Leading his donkey into the enclosed yard, he tied the beast and began unloading the heavy baskets. Little James, as he was called, was three inches under five feet, but his shoulders and arms were muscled like a man of greater stature.

The unloading was finished and the heavy clay was safely on the ground. James found a piece of rough cloth and carefully rubbed the donkey's dark coat dry. From a small shed in the corner he brought hay and placed it in front of the beast next to a bucket of water. Now he was free to look after his own wants. He went inside and was greeted by the older woman who had opened the door for him.

"It grieves me to see you struggle with those heavy baskets of clay all by yourself, James. It's too much for one man—especially . . ." The woman paused, noticing the frown flitting across the face of the man she addressed.

"Especially a little man—a man not five feet tall! That's what you meant to say, isn't it?" asked James. His tone was not harsh and there was no bitterness in his voice.

"No! Yes, yes, it's true I was going to say especially a small man. And yet my meaning was not what it sounds. Oh, James—my son, you are not small to me. It's only a mother's way to want to protect the son she loves. I wish your father were still here and Joses had not moved away."

"James-the-Less, they call me—Little James. I do not mind. I've learned the small man's role. And yet my dreams are no

166

small dreams. I dream dreams a giant would be proud to own. But they are only dreams, and I still spin the potter's wheel and travel to Capernaum to sell clay pots and jugs and lamps!" The small man laughed aloud. His mother turned away and busied herself with preparing the evening meal.

James washed his hands free from the clay in which he worked and walked outside to look at the last rays of sun setting over Galilee. It was true he did dream brave dreams, but he never shared them with others. His father had been a good man. He had taught James not to be sensitive about his small stature. Always, even as a boy, James had been treated as an equal by his father and by his older brother, Joses. Gradually the taunts of his school-mates had faded from James's ears. He learned to do whatever he set out to do. His name would always be James-the-Less, Little James, but by the time his father died he had grown to manhood and proved his worth. When his brother married and moved to Cana, James was left alone to look after his mother. He was still called Little James, but by now "little" was a friendly word.

Every two weeks or so James traveled the long day's journey to Capernaum. There he sold his load of pottery, and when he was through he made the journey home again. It was on these trips James thought of his ambitions. The first time he had made the trip with his father, they followed the road along the shore when they reached the Sea of Galilee. James had seen the fishing boats. He had watched some fishermen out testing a new sail. He saw the wind fill the white sail and send the small boat skimming along the blue water. From that moment on he had wanted to work with boats. Whenever he could spare time from the market place on his trips to Capernaum, he went down to the shore and watched the boats.

So James dreamed of his ambition to be a fisherman, to own boats and sail them on the blue Sea of Galilee. He knew it was an impossible dream. He was bound to a potter's wheel in Nain.

Even had he been free to learn the fisherman's trade, his small stature would have kept him from his goal. He was just not tall enough to handle the long, heavy oar.

The tall net-mender bent over his task. He was so absorbed in trying to finish mending the hole in the net that the man who watched him remained unnoticed for some minutes. Suddenly the man mending the net looked up. Opposite him he saw a short man holding the halter of a donkey and staring at him.

"Have you never seen a net being mended before?" asked the net-mender sullenly. This was the job he liked least, and the tear he was mending was a particularly difficult one to mend. To add to his bad temper his brother had been called away. The job of mending the net was John's to do alone.

"No, I never have seen a net mended before. Is it difficult? Do you mind if I watch or do you want me to leave?" The little man started to lead his donkey away. He could tell from the surly tone of the net-mender his presence wasn't welcome.

"Stay, if you like. This is the job I like least about fishing and this tear is the worst one yet. I suppose that's why I sounded so angry when I spoke to you." John looked up and smiled. Just as he looked up, he jabbed his finger with the tool he was using to mend the net.

"Oh-h!" he exclaimed, putting his finger to his mouth. "I'm always doing that. My brother calls me John-the-Clumsy. I've just shown you why he calls me so. By the way, how are you called?"

"My name is James and I'm called James-the-Less or Little James by most people. You can see why," James answered.

"Little James! Yes, you're shorter than most men, it's true. My brother's name is James. What trade do you follow, Little James? I know you're not a fisherman, for all fishermen in Galilee know each other."

168

"I'm a potter," sighed James. "Little James, the potter of Nain. I've sold my wares at the marketplace. Now I'm bound for home. I've always loved to watch the sea and the boats. Whenever I sell my pots and jugs quickly enough, I come here to watch a while before starting back to Nain."

"You love the sea and I would rather be almost anything than a fisherman. It's strange we two should meet," said John, turning again to his net with a frown.

"Can I help you with that?" asked James. "I've been watching you and I think I know how."

"I'll be glad of any help you can give," answered John. "This isn't the best part of fishing. It's the part I like least."

Quickly the deft fingers of the little potter knotted the cords and helped John place the new cords so that the great tear seemed to close like magic. John's eyes opened in amazement at the skill his new friend showed in mending the net.

"I can't believe you never mended nets before. I've been doing this since I was a boy and you've twice the skill I have. You'd be worth having in our crew just to mend the nets!" exclaimed John fervently.

Little James smiled with pleasure at the words. "It isn't really hard. You don't like to do it and that makes it harder for you. This is as close as I'll ever get to being a fisherman. You don't like fishing and I dream of something better than a potter's wheel. Maybe someday both our dreams will come true."

The small man stood up. He walked over to where he had tethered his donkey. The net was mended. It was time to start the journey back to Nain.

The tall net-mender named John lifted his hand in a farewell sign. "Thanks, small potter, for your help. Come and visit me when you come to Capernaum again."

"Perhaps I will." James waved his hand and started on the journey home.

I'll Find a Way to Grow

There was no main road between Nain and Cana, so the donkey with the two huge clay wine vessels—one strapped on either side—had to follow the trails and footpaths. His master picked the way carefully. The message had been urgent. The son of a prominent man in Cana was getting married. Preparations for the wedding feast had been in progress for days. The steward had discovered cracks in two of the wine vessels. A hurried call was sent to the potter of Nain to bring new vessels, and quickly. The new vessels would be needed for the wedding feast.

James-the-Less had done his work and the new vessels were carefully loaded on the donkey. Now he was bound for Cana. He was glad to have the opportunity to go. His older brother, Joses, lived in Cana, and he would have an opportunity to visit with his brother when the wine vessels had been delivered. Walking along with only his donkey for company, James sang to himself. He often made up songs and sang them to himself when he was alone. Digging the heavy clay from the clay pits, stoking the fire in the kiln where the pottery was baked—everything about the potter's work was hard, but James found many things to sing about. His voice was deep and powerful and carried a long way. Today he was singing one of his favorite songs. It was one he had made up long ago. It went like this:

> "They call me James-the-Less,
> But they don't know me well.
> I'm really James-the-Tall!
> My voice rings like a bell.
> And in my dreams, I jump King Herod's wall.
> But only in my dreams do I find happiness."

The little man paused and then began the second verse of his song.

"I'm twice the man they think I am,
For Little James is not so small.
Someday I'll find a way to grow,
And be ten cubits tall!
Someday I'll find a way to grow,
And they'll call me James-the-Man!"

James-the-Less was small, but just as his song said, his voice *did* ring like a bell. His powerful voice rang through the little valley ahead of him. It could be clearly heard by a small group of travelers who rested just around a bend in the road. James checked his singing as he saw the group. He was about to put his head down and hurry by to hide his embarrassment and get away from the taunting he expected. Suddenly he recognized one of the group. The tall, thin young man came striding up to him.

"That's a brave song you sing, James-the-Less. You sing it well. Did you make up the words yourself?" It was his friend John the net-mender who came up to him.

"I'm alone a good deal. Sometimes when I'm by myself I make up songs and sing them. I didn't think anyone was around," answered James.

"Don't worry about that. We enjoyed hearing you sing. Come meet my Master and my friends." John urged the potter over to where Jesus sat with Simon, Andrew, James-bar-Zebedee, and Matthew.

"Master, this is James-the-Less, the potter of Nain. We met in Capernaum and he helped me mend a net even though he had never tried it before. I've never seen a man so clever with his fingers. He may be small but he learns quickly."

"I heard your song, James. I think you *will* find a way to grow." Jesus smiled at the small man who looked even shorter standing

171

beside the tall fisherman at his side. Then James met each of the others in turn.

"We're going to a wedding here in Cana," explained John. "We have plenty of time, and Philip, one of our number, is visiting a friend of his while we rest here and wait for him."

"That reminds me that I'd better hurry," replied James-the-Less. "I'm delivering these new wine vessels to the bridegroom's home. I must hurry." James waved good-bye and pulled at his donkey's halter. He was not far from the home of the bridegroom. The rest of the way he thought of the man John had referred to as Master. The calm voice that was so warm and alive. "I think you will find a way to grow." The small man smiled to himself and his heart beat more quickly. He didn't know why, but somehow he felt taller already.

Ten Cubits Tall

Joses looked at his brother beside him. He could not help smiling as he listened to James tell his story of meeting with his friend and being introduced to his friend's leader and the other members of the group. He had told Joses about the song he was singing and how the leader had said to him, "I think you will find a way to grow, James."

"Do you really believe he meant what he said, Joses? Do you really think it's possible for a man to grow after he's reached manhood?" asked James.

"Jesus of Nazareth is known as a wise teacher. I have never

heard him speak, but I have heard of him. His fame is just becoming known throughout Galilee. From all I have heard he would say only what he really believed, James. I have heard he says things that are sometimes difficult to understand." Joses shook his head and went back to cultivating soil around his young olive trees. His brother picked up his hoe and began helping. It was good to be with Joses again. He had missed his brother. Joses had never called him Little James, but the difference in their sizes had made it certain that the younger brother would be called Little James. He remembered when his brother had decided to move to Cana and live there with his wife's mother. James had been glad. With Joses gone, perhaps he wouldn't be called Little James anymore, he had thought. But the name hadn't changed, and he missed the company of his brother. That was when he had first made up the song he had been singing.

James-the-Less felt ashamed as he remembered how he had been glad when his brother had left Nain. As if to make up for it he began to work harder than before. Moving from tree to tree, he loosened the earth and broke the larger clods so that all the soil around the young trees was loosened and broken into small particles. Now when the rain came the roots of the young olive trees would get every drop of moisture. None would run off and be wasted. He worked so steadily he moved well away from his slower, more methodical older brother. He didn't notice the running figure of his brother's wife coming toward them. It was only when she shouted he knew something was wrong.

"Joses, Joses, come quickly! Something has happened to Hannah!"

James was too far away to hear all his sister-in-law had shouted, but he could tell something was wrong and he threw down his hoe and ran to find out. Mara, his sister-in-law, told what had happened between sobs. Hannah, the three-year-old, had somehow escaped her mother's eye for a few minutes. The little girl had been playing

173

near the house and then suddenly she was gone. Mara had searched everywhere and then she had heard faint cries. The very worst had happened. Hannah had fallen into the abandoned well.

Already Joses and James were hurrying toward the house. Years ago Mara's father had had the well dug and it had supplied water for many years. At last it had gone dry and been abandoned. The stone wall which surrounded the well had fallen into disrepair and some of the stones had loosened and fallen into the well, leaving an opening in the wall. Somehow Hannah had crawled through this breach and fallen into the well.

The shaft of the well was deep but small in diameter. The well had been designed only to serve the needs of Mara's family, and in the years of disuse the side had become faulty. Even if there was a rope long enough, Hannah was too small to help herself. Her cries told those above she was still alive, but she might be injured. Perhaps badly. Joses tried to calm his wife for a moment and then he spoke to James: "Stay here and do what you can for Mara. I'm going to my neighbors to get help." With those words Joses left, running as fast as he could go.

Already James was taking off cloak and tunic. He took off his sandals. Next he tore his tunic in half and fashioned a loose sling which he knotted around his neck so that the sling hung down his back. He tore his cloak into strips, knotting each strip carefully to the next one. If I were taller, he thought, my strips would be longer. He found the halter for his donkey and added that to his hastily contrived rope. Seeing what he was doing, Mara dried her tears and ran to the house. Quickly she returned with coverings from the beds. The rope grew longer and longer. Was it long enough? They had used all they had to make the rope. What they had would have to do.

Mara looked down the well while James made his preparations. A little speck of white was all she saw. The opening was so small. There would be no room to turn. She doubted even James could

174

find a way. Hannah cried again and Mara turned away. She could not bear to look.

James led his old friend the donkey to the edge of the well. He tied the halter end of the rope around the donkey's neck and made sure the knot was secure. He talked to Mara and in a dozen words explained his plan. Now he knotted the other end of the rope around his own ankles. He bound them as close together as he could.

Mara led the donkey away from the well. At last James called to her to stop. The distance was far enough. James, with the sling around his neck, went head first into the narrow well, his arms extended. Slowly Mara led the donkey toward the well and the small potter made his slow, head-first descent. He felt his skull would burst as the blood rushed to his head. Even for his small frame the narrow shaft of the well was close. His shoulders scraped on either side. The hard dirt and limestone scraped his arms and shoulders raw. He wore only his linen underpants. Where the shaft widened slightly, his head bumped against an outcropping of rock. The halter rope which bound his ankles cut into his flesh. Lower into the well he slowly moved. It was hard to see with the blood pounding in his temples, and his body obscured the little light that penetrated from above. The speck of white grew larger at the bottom of the well. There was no cry.

The shaft narrowed. Little James was stuck fast. The rope slackened behind him. He tried to call out, but he was too tightly stuck. Where was the voice that rang like a bell, he asked himself. There was only one thing to do. With a mighty twist which tore the skin from shoulders already rubbed raw, James freed himself. Now he dropped free and his head grazed the wall of the well. The blood sang in his head, but his fingers touched something small and warm. He gripped the small warm bundle, but best of all he heard a cry. Somehow James was able to shout. He felt the pull on his ankles. Slowly he was being pulled back to the surface.

Hannah was safe in his sling. Between the weight around his neck and the pull on his ankles James felt his very bones were being stretched.

They were all running as fast as they could. Joses, his neighbors, even the teacher from Nazareth with his followers on the way to Capernaum hastened back with Joses to see if they could help. They arrived just in time to help pull James-the-Less from the well. Hannah was crying and bruised, but that was all. The dirt and debris at the bottom of the well had broken her fall. James-the-Less was a different matter. He was unconscious. The skin of his upper arms and shoulders was rubbed raw, and blood and dirt mixed in the ugly wounds. His head was bruised and bleeding. A circle of chafed skin told where the rope had bound his ankles. Tenderly Joses carried his brother to the house. Mara and Joses washed and bound the wounds.

The little man awakened and groaned. He opened his eyes. He saw his brother and Mara bending over him. Joses answered the question in his brother's eyes.

"Hannah is well, James. You saved her. No one else could have done what you did. No one else would have had the quick wit and courage."

James smiled, and then he heard the voice which made him forget his wounds.

"Remember, I told you that you would find a way to grow. You've grown tall enough today for any man, James." The teacher from Nazareth was speaking to him. James felt a glow inside he'd never felt before. Suddenly he was ten cubits tall. Now he knew what the teacher from Nazareth had meant when he talked to him before. Now he knew what being tall really meant. It was hard to speak, but James managed a husky whisper.

"Master, am I tall enough to serve with you?" he asked.

"Yes, James. You're tall enough. Join us in Capernaum when you are well." The tall Nazarene turned away and motioned to the others to come away and let James rest. Even though he ached in every muscle, James had never felt so well.

James-the-Tall

"The tomb is empty. He has risen!" His mother threw her arms around him and embraced him. James was stunned. Then at last the words of his mother penetrated his dullness. It was not the end of everything after all! He was not just a little man less than five feet tall who had followed a dream.

When James had met Jesus and become one of the disciples, it was as if he had grown to the height he had always yearned for. He was small in size, but there was nothing small about his heart. He had thrown himself into the work Jesus had given him. When Jesus had sent the disciples out in pairs, James-the-Less and Thaddaeus had gone together. The small man's voice attracted the attention of the crowds and he had been able to prove being small of stature was not a handicap.

Like the others, he had not heeded the hints Jesus had given them of what was to come. That night in Gethsemane had stunned James. He could not think clearly. The next day he had watched in the crowd near Simon Zelotes. He saw the big man slip away when the crowd shouted for Barabbas to be freed. James had gone away too. He could not even bear to join his mother as she watched with the other women on the hill called Calvary. Like a wounded animal

177

he had gone off by himself, too wrapped in his own grief to think clearly. At times he slept, only to wake from a fitful slumber and brood on the death of his beloved Master. The night passed, and the next day. The following morning he rose and went seeking his mother. He needed human companionship.

Somehow she at the same time was seeking him. And then she had found him with the good news. James hurried to see the others. Jesus had risen from the tomb!

The disciples had spread in many directions to take the good news to all parts of the civilized world. James-the-Less was assigned to stay in Jerusalem and help the struggling church there. In many ways it was the most difficult of all assignments, because in Jerusalem the jealousy of the Sanhedrin and the high priest backed a well-organized and continuing opposition to the early church.

The agents of the high priest were everywhere in Jerusalem. Some said Caiaphas, the high priest, had ears in every wall. James and others of the disciples and their followers were often in the Temple. This was the gathering place where people talked about the issues of the day and discussed philosophy and religion.

James-the-Less was there talking to some of those who had been followers of Jesus and who had remained faithful to his teachings through the encouragement of the disciples. Agents of Caiaphas saw their chance to win favor with the high priest and dispose of James as well. Rudely they burst in where James was talking to a group of his followers in a corner of the outer court.

"This man is a fraud," shouted the leader. "He blasphemes our sacred Temple with his teachings. The man he says was the Messias is dead. He was crucified as a criminal. How can you listen to him!"

"Jesus Christ rose from the grave. He talked and showed himself to all of us who worked with him. Your lies cannot change things. Only men such as you blaspheme," replied James.

178

The high priest's man shouted an oath and drew his sword. At once some of James's followers prepared to fight and gathered themselves in front of James.

"No, no. We must not fight," cried James. "Jesus taught us that those who live by the sword also perish by the sword. He would not have his followers strike any man." Turning his back on his tormentors, James pushed his followers back, and then so that he might speak to them all and so they could hear him more clearly, he climbed the steps above them and stood there on the highest step alone.

It was too good a chance for the leader of the high priest's men to miss. Sword in hand, with his followers at his back, the leader climbed the steps and thrust upward with his sword. For a moment James stood erect. Slowly he fell. Even in falling, he seemed taller than any there.

THADDAEUS
Who Followed the Star

The night was chill in the Judean foothills where Thaddaeus watched the sheep with Azriel, his uncle, and the other shepherds. Watching the stars in the dark sky, Thaddaeus wondered how it could be so warm during the day and so cool at night. But when you're ten years old, there are no end of things to wonder about. He fingered the willow whistle in his pocket and placed it to his lips. Softly he played a tune. It was a tune he had heard his mother hum many times when he was small.

The tune stirred memories. Abruptly he put his willow whistle back in his pocket and began to think of his home in Galilee. Everything here was so different from Bethsaida. At Bethsaida there had been the blue water and games along the shore. There had been the excitement of seeing the fishing fleet depart and the excitement when the catch was good. There had been dread times as well, when the wind swept down the valley of the Jordan and the white waves lashed the Sea of Galilee. Remembering, Thaddaeus shivered. Such a storm was why he was here in this country so new and strange to him.

The evening had been calm enough when the fishing boats set out. There had not been a cloud in the sky all day. In the early evening the red ball of sun dipped over the hills on the western shore. The boats were ready to set out. Ezra, the father of Thaddaeus, pulled at his oar with the others. His wife and small son waved from the shore. All went well that evening until almost time to start back. The fishing had been better than usual. The boats were two-thirds full and still an hour's fishing remained.

Suddenly the wind changed. The long, slow rolls in the sea became short and choppy. All fishing stopped. Each fisherman bent his ear to the west. The low, moaning sound grew louder. At once the fishermen burst into furious activity. Nets were hauled in as quickly as possible. Sails were tightly furled. Now each oarsman bent to his work as if his life depended on each stroke he took— and that was so. If they were caught against the western wall of rock rising sheer and straight from the sea, it meant the end of boats and men.

The heavy-laden boats made slow progress, but gradually they pulled their way to the center of this inland sea. Now screaming down at them the west wind flung its might. These men had fought the wind before. They did not give up easily. No faint heart ever fished in Galilee. Ezra, first oarsman on the left, caught the full force of the wind but bent to the heavy oar and put his full weight into the pull. The small boat moved ahead like some giant turtle slowly inching through the rough water. Perhaps the blade of the oar struck a trifle deep. Maybe the oarsman hurried his stroke and placed a sudden strain upon his oar. In any case the bow oars-

181

man on the right snapped his blade! Instantly the boat lost headway, turned, and jerked the left oarsman forward and hurled him into the bow of the boat. Only the lull between the heavy gusts of wind saved the boat. In those seconds when the wind abated, the spare oar always carried for just such an emergency was passed to the man who had broken his oar.

One of the net-handlers huddled near the mast crawled quickly to take Ezra's oar. The next gust came, and others after them, but now the fury of the storm had spent itself. Battered men and storm-tossed boat made it to the shore. Sadly the crewmen carried the unconscious form of Ezra to his home.

The days went by and slowly the injured man began to mend. Arm and shoulder bones were broken. And there were ribs to mend as well. It would be long, if ever, before Ezra could fish again. Ezra's brother lived nearby. He could make room for two, but not an inch of space remained to house and feed another.

So the decision was made and word was sent to Judea. Then the answer came from Thaddaeus' mother's brother:—"Send the boy. I'll care for him until his father is well again." Arrangements were made for the lad to make the journey with trusted friends. It was the time of the Passover feast when many made the trip to Jerusalem. The boy's uncle would meet him there. And so it came about.

Now on this quiet night with his warm cloak drawn around him the boy remembered Galilee and all his friends. The night was cool, but he shivered because of a west wind which had blown months ago and now blew in his memory again. He wished he could go home. Azriel was very kind and treated Thaddaeus as if he were his own son. The son he'd never had, for Azriel had never married. The shepherd owned large flocks of sheep. There were at least five hundred sheep—counting the new lambs—in this flock. Azriel hired shepherds to watch with him as they grazed the flock. It was all new and interesting, but still Thaddaeus was homesick.

He liked the nights best. It was then he listened as the shepherds

182

told their tales to pass the lonely hours while they kept watch in turn. These quiet men told tales of kings and princes from far lands to set the boy's head spinning as he listened in delight. And there were tales of how the wolves attacked, and of strange things that happened in the night. The men watched the boy's eyes grow big and smiled among themselves and turned their talk to gentler things. The fire burned low and Thaddaeus' eyes began to close. Azriel found a blanket. He wrapped the boy warmly and watched him as he slept. Then Azriel lay down beside him and let the shepherds keep the watch.

The willow whistle Azriel had made was Thaddaeus' favorite plaything. His uncle taught him how to pipe a shepherd's tune and use it to call the sheep when some adventurous animal strayed too far from the main flock. One day he lost the whistle, and though he searched everywhere he could not find it.

"I'll show you how to make a whistle, Thaddaeus. Then when you lose it you can make yourself another. It isn't hard to do." Azriel cut a small branch from a willow tree. He peeled the bark away and placed it on a rock in the sun to dry. Two days he let it dry in the sun. Then he cut two lengths from the branch.

"See, each whistle is about a span in length." The shepherd measured with his hand. "From tip of thumb to tip of little finger is a span. Spread your hand as wide as it will go. Remember one span is half a cubit." Azriel took his knife and gently hollowed out the pithy willow wood. Next he measured with the first joint of his thumb. Two thumb joints from one end he began to cut an opening in the length of hollow willow. Carefully he cut the opening square. A thumb joint farther down he cut another, and then a third. Thaddaeus watched his uncle carefully.

"Why do you make openings square, Azriel?" he asked. "All the other shepherds have round holes in their whistles."

"The square holes make a slightly different sound. I suppose it's just one man's way of making his own mark, Thaddaeus," Azriel answered him "I always cut mine square. When you see square holes in a willow whistle, you'll know Azriel's knife did the work." His uncle smiled and tossed the finished whistle to the boy.

"Let me make one and I'll give the one I make to you," said Thaddaeus. He worked as carefully as he could, holding it up for his uncle to see as he hollowed out the length of wood. He began to cut the openings, measuring carefully as he had seen his uncle do. Square holes were harder to cut than round ones, and the first opening was a little crooked. Gradually Thaddaeus got the hang of it and the next two openings were square and neat.

Azriel smiled. "This is the first whistle anyone ever made for me. I'll play a tune for you." He blew into his whistle, and sure enough the sound came clear and sweet.

The days went on and the nights became more chill. Soon it would be time to head the flock for Jerusalem and the market there.

The night was very dark. There was no moon at all. The stars were scattered in the sky and seemed fewer than usual, Thaddaeus noticed. He sat well back from the fire to keep the firelight from his eyes so he could watch the outline of the flock and tell when a sheep stirred for any reason. It was a shepherd's trick he'd learned from his uncle. It was later than he usually stayed up. Only Thaddaeus and the two shepherds whose turn it was to watch were still awake.

Thaddaeus lay on his back and looked at the dark sky. It seemed to grow lighter in the east, but that couldn't be. It was much too early for dawn, and tonight there was no moon. Moonrise had been long past, anyway. The light became brighter. Could it be a star? A star as bright as this, and moving east? Thaddaeus sat up and rubbed his eyes. No, he hadn't been dreaming! He stood up. He could hear the shepherds on watch talking. Now he saw them point to the star. They too had seen what he had seen. Thaddaeus ran to awaken his uncle.

184

"Azriel, Azriel, wake up. Something strange is happening!" Thaddaeus shook his uncle by the arm. The older man quickly awoke. Thaddaeus pointed to the sky. "Look," he said, "the brightest star I've ever seen!"

His uncle gazed up at the bright star moving east ahead of them. "It's the star of the ancient stories," he said. "It's the King's star, the star of the legend!"

"What star is that?" asked Thaddaeus.

"The old stories say one night a star will appear in the east— the brightest star in all the heavens. The star will lead the way to where a King is born. The King who will lead Israel to all the glory our country once had."

"Then we must follow the star and find the King," cried Thaddaeus.

Azriel watched the bright star above in silence for a while. He was thinking to himself. Could it *really* be the star he had heard about? Would it really lead them to where a King was born? At last he nodded his head and looked at Thaddaeus. "Yes, we must follow the star! Come, I'll wake Kish and Ohad. They'll go with us. We'll leave the others to tend the flock." Azriel hurried off to wake the two shepherds who had been with him since the time he had begun his flock.

The three shepherds and the small boy prepared to leave.

"Wait," Ohad said. "We can't go to a King empty-handed!"

"Select the three finest lambs we have," ordered Azriel. "Each of us will take a fine lamb. It's the best we have. Surely the King will accept our gift." Kish and Ohad nodded and went to bring the lambs.

Thaddaeus felt a little sad. He'd made friends with the lambs. He liked watching them run and play. Sometimes he would hold one and stroke the soft wool. Still, a King should have a gift, and these lambs were the best gifts they could offer. Walking along beside Azriel and looking up at the lamb in the tall shepherd's

185

arms, Thaddaeus wished he had a gift to bring. He had nothing you could offer to a King.

They walked for several hours, and then in the gray light before dawn the small group slept on the open ground. The sun was up when they awoke, but the white light of the star still shone in the sky. The star moved slowly now. The little group pressed on.

"It moved toward Bethlehem!" exclaimed Azriel in the afternoon as they rested. "It must be the star of the legend. A King born in a stable in Bethlehem. I remember now." And so they walked. In the late evening they came to Bethlehem, and over the small town the star shone bright and did not move. Down the narrow streets the shepherds searched, each carrying in his arms a lamb. At last, back of the inn, they found a stable. It was a large cave cut into the hillside behind the inn.

Azriel led the way. Behind him Kish and Ohad followed. A man and a woman knelt on either side of a small manger where straw had been placed and covered with a blanket. In the manger a baby lay kicking his small feet in the air and making the noises babies make. Azriel moved to the foot of the manger and, kneeling, placed the sleepy little lamb there.

"A present for the King," he said. "We followed the star from where we watched our flocks. We bring the best we have." The parents of the child smiled and thanked him for his gift. In turn the two other shepherds brought their lambs and placed them by the manger.

Thaddaeus watched from the entrance to the stable. He wished he had a gift to bring. He placed his hand in the pocket of his cloak. His hand closed on the willow whistle Azriel had made for him. He drew it out and looked at it. It was only a whistle, but boys liked whistles. Looking at the whistle in his hand, he fingered the square openings for a moment. Then he walked quickly to the manger. Gently he placed the whistle on the blanket covering the baby. A tiny finger touched the slender length of willow and it

186

rolled out of reach. The baby's mother looked at Thaddaeus and smiled. Quickly he went back to the entrance. Already Azriel with Kish and Ohad had turned to go. Thaddaeus looked back. The baby seemed so small to be a King.

A Willow Whistle

The hills above Capernaum were lush with grass. The rains this spring had been heavier than most times, and the grass was thicker than usual. It was for this reason Thaddaeus grazed his sheep closer to the city. Later on he would have to move to the higher slopes, but now there was plenty of grass here on the edge of the city.

As usual, children were around. Thaddaeus was popular with the children. He told them stories and they liked to watch the lambs. Sometimes he would let them pick up a lamb and hold it in their arms. Some boy or girl was always asking for a whistle. Thaddaeus made many for the children of Capernaum and taught them how to play tunes as well.

A shepherd's life was often lonely, and Thaddaeus liked the company of the children. Later in the summer, when he climbed higher in the hills, he would miss the children. Now, while the grass was still plentiful along the main road on the outskirts of Capernaum, he was enjoying the children and watching the passers-by along the road. Watching the children play with the lambs made Thaddaeus remember his own boyhood.

The foothills of Judea were different from the hills of Galilee but a shepherd's life was much the same. He had learned the shepherd's way from his uncle, Azriel. For three years he had lived with his uncle and learned the shepherd's skills. Then word had come from Bethsaida. His father had recovered from his injuries. Ezra would never fish again, but father and son working together could take care of a flock of sheep. So father had learned from son, and together they built up the flock and grazed the hills outside Capernaum with their sheep. When his father died Thaddaeus continued the shepherd's life, looking after his mother and spending most of his time alone with his flock. After his mother's death he came to the city only for supplies or to sell some of his sheep. It was a lonely life, but occasionally he had the children of the city for company and he enjoyed telling them stories. For some reason he never told the story of following the star. He didn't know why he kept that story hidden in his heart. Had the babe he saw in the manger really been the King who would bring back the glory of Israel? Thaddaeus didn't know. He was in his forties now. His beard was beginning to turn gray. Judea seemed so far away. The years had passed him by.

The small group paused to rest under a tree by the side of the road. Curious as always, the children left Thaddaeus to see who the strangers by the roadside were. One of the half-dozen got up as the children approached and cautioned them to go on with their playing somewhere else. "Our Master has been walking a long way. He needs to rest undisturbed," the man said. The children turned, but before they could go the leader of the group spoke up.

"Simon-bar-Jonah, let the children come," he said. "They don't disturb me and I like to talk with them." And so the children gathered round, and soon the air was full of questions, laughter, and merry shouts. One lad pulled a whistle from his pocket and played a lively tune. The man who had called the children to his side listened to the whistle carefully and held out his hand.

"May I see your whistle?" he asked.

188

The lad who owned the whistle gave a final trill and dropped his whistle in the outstretched hand. Carefully the man looked at the whistle, fingering the square openings cut in the peeled willow tube. "I owned a whistle such as this," he said. "It was long ago. I lost it the way boys lose playthings."

"I know," the boy replied. "This is the third one Thaddaeus has made for me."

"And all the whistles that he makes are like this one?" the boy's new friend asked.

"Oh, yes," the boy answered. "He makes them all alike. He told us once his uncle taught him how a long time ago. Thaddaeus is just over there with his sheep." The boy pointed to where Thaddaeus watched his sheep a hundred yards away.

The tall man stood up. "Stay here and talk with my friends," he told the children. "I'll bring your whistle back. I want to talk to the shepherd for a moment."

Thaddaeus looked up and saw the tall man coming toward him. He was no one he had ever seen before, and yet he felt that he should know him.

"You're Thaddaeus, the children tell me. I understand you make whistles for them?" the stranger said.

"Yes, I'm called Thaddaeus, right enough. I enjoy the children, and sometimes to entertain them I make whistles and teach them how to play a tune. Why do you ask?"

"Once long ago someone gave me a whistle. I lost it like all boys lose things. My father made another one, and many more after that, but only the first one was like this." The stranger opened his hand and placed the whistle in Thaddaeus' hand.

"It's only a common willow whistle," Thaddaeus replied. "What's different about this one?"

"The openings are square," answered the stranger. "All the other whistles have round holes for the openings."

Thaddaeus jumped up in quick amazement. "The little King!"

189

he exclaimed. "I placed my whistle on the blanket near his hand! We had followed the star from where we watched our flocks. I was only a lad no bigger than those playing yonder. My uncle and his shepherds were there. We followed the star to Bethlehem to find the King! The whistle was all I had to give." Thaddaeus dropped to his knees and bowed his head.

"I am called Jesus of Nazareth by my friends. Stand here beside me, Thaddaeus. My mother treasured all the gifts that came to me there in the stable in Bethlehem. There came a time when I was old enough to play with the whistle you brought as a gift. And now we meet again."

"To stand beside a King, a shepherd standing beside a King." Thaddaeus breathed the words softly.

"My kingdom is not of this world, Thaddaeus," Jesus replied.

"Lord, may I serve you? Is there something such a one as I can do to be part of your company?" Thaddaeus hardly dared to ask, and yet he knew his heart would burst unless he did.

"I want you to be one of my twelve, Thaddaeus. Will you continue to follow the star no matter where it leads?" Jesus looked at the shepherd and took the whistle from his hand. "Someday you'll make another one for me. I must return this one to its owner. Come, Thaddaeus, follow me."

Follow the Star

"Lord, how is it that you show yourself to us but yet you do not show all the world you are the chosen one?" Thaddaeus asked the question because he was troubled again. He often had difficulty understanding Jesus' words. Once again he had heard but had not understood. It was the Passover supper they were celebrating together in the upper room John and Peter had arranged. Jesus had talked to the disciples at length. Jesus had said: "In a little while the world will see me no more, but you will see me. And because I live you will live also. He who loves me shall be loved by my Father and I will love him and show myself to him."

It was in response to this statement Thaddaeus had asked his question. Jesus was the chosen one. The King who would bring back the glory of Israel. Thaddaeus could not forget that night as a boy when Azriel had told him the story of the star. The star will guide us to the King, his uncle had told him, and Thaddaeus believed. He would always believe. He couldn't understand why Jesus had not already claimed Israel for his own. Surely the time was soon.

Slowly Jesus answered Thaddaeus. "You still do not understand, Thaddaeus. Don't you remember what I said long ago, 'My kingdom is not of this world'? If a man loves me and believes in what I have taught, my Father will love that man. We will enter into his spirit and be with him always."

Thaddaeus listened carefully and nodded his head, but the puzzled look was still there. There was so much to learn and to understand.

The road to Edessa from Jerusalem was very long, for Edessa lay far, far to the north across the great desert. But Edessa itself was a pleasant city with the land made fertile by the overflow of the Tigris when the snow melted in the mountains and the rains came. It had taken a long time to make the journey, but now Thaddaeus had arrived. He began his work. Tobias, the man he had been instructed to call upon, took him in and received him with a warm welcome. Thaddaeus began by telling the small groups who would listen to him the good news of the coming of Jesus and what he had taught. Jesus had been crucified and had risen from the dead and then had ascended to heaven. And always Thaddaeus told of how, as a boy, he himself had followed the star to the stable in Bethlehem.

Thaddaeus was not a learned man, but he spoke so sincerely and with such conviction the people listened to him. Abgarus the King heard of Thaddaeus and called him to his palace and listened to Thaddaeus tell the story of Jesus. Abgarus was so impressed he promised to call all his people together and have them listen while Thaddaeus told the story of Jesus as he had told it to Abgarus.

"I will preach to them and tell the word of God concerning the coming of Jesus, of how he was born, of his mission on earth. I will tell them about the power of his words and how, though he humbled himself on the cross, he rose again and ascended to heaven to be with his Father. All these things I will tell them and many more," Thaddaeus told Abgarus.

For many years Thaddaeus labored in Edessa, and his teachings took root and the church began to grow. After some years he returned to Jerusalem and worked there, but the old longing to take the teachings of Jesus to other people came to him again. He remembered it was his destiny to "follow the star." Long ago he had promised to follow the star no matter where it led. He must keep the promise.

So once again he made the long journey, and this time he traveled to even more remote country than before. To the far region of Armenia, where Mount Ararat reared its head to the clouds, Thaddaeus traveled.

Always his story was the same. The story of Jesus, the King who had been born in a stable. The King who had come not to claim a kingdom but to teach the world about a new kingdom where all who believed in his teachings might someday dwell.

192

There in the wild regions of Mount Ararat were some who listened, but this was the holy mountain of people who believed in strange gods. Some became angry at the man who spoke of the one true God and his son Jesus Christ who had lived on earth, had died and risen from the dead again. Some of the chief men muttered to themselves: "If this man is holy, let his God raise him from the dead if he can." It was agreed. One day Thaddaeus told the story about how Jesus had been born in a stable and how Thaddaeus himself had, as a lad, followed the star to Bethlehem. As he spoke, an arrow winged through the trees and struck him in the heart. Thaddaeus fell dead. He had followed the star to Bethlehem again.

SIMON PETER
Fisherman of Galilee

At last Simon and his wife, Lois, were alone. It was very late. Simon, Andrew, James, and John had talked for hours with Jesus on the shore. Slowly to his wife Simon related all that had happened. He told her of meeting Jesus and how angry Zebedee had been.

"You can't really blame Zebedee for being so angry, Simon. To lose all four of you at once, and without warning. It will be hard for him to hire others who can replace you four. Is this really what you must do?"

"There is no other way, wife. I must follow Jesus. There on the shore as we sat and listened to him I felt I must be going mad. Simon-bar-Jonah throwing down his nets to follow a new teacher!

194

You knew me as a lad. Do you remember? I could not wait till I was old enough to take a place in my father's boat. How I begged him for the chance! Fishing is what I've always wanted to do. With me it has been more than just a way to earn our bread. It's been my life. And now, in an instant, I've turned my back on all I have ever known or wanted because he turned his eyes on me and said, 'Follow me.' I do not understand it, Lois. I do not understand myself. Have I gone mad?"

"Oh, no, Simon, you've not gone mad. You are the same Simon I have always known and loved. This is no new thing for you to make up your mind in an instant. This Jesus, whoever he may be, is surely worthy of your trust. You must follow him. In following him, you follow your old instinct for quick decisions. I do not yet know Jesus, but I know my Simon. If you must follow him, his way must surely be the one true path for you. I would have you be true to your own heart however hard it may be for you and for me." Lois turned to her husband and the fisherman held his wife close. There were no more words. The wonder was those burly arms, accustomed to straining at the nets, could become so gentle at another time.

The next day the four new disciples went to the synagogue in Capernaum, and it was there Simon and the other three heard Jesus preach and tell how God loved all men. Then Lois' mother was cured of a high fever when Jesus simply touched her. Now Lois too put her own trust in Jesus. Simon, Andrew, James, and John left the fishing fleet and followed Jesus.

Lois often followed to listen to Jesus talk to the crowds when she could. Old Zebedee would have no part of Jesus or his sons' new work, but Salome often followed them when the way was not too far. Lois went with her, when she could, leaving her mother to look after the children. As she had said to Simon, the way was hard for both of them. Simon put all of his energy into his work, but there were times when he longed to feel the cool breeze in his face and sink the big drift net in the blue water. There were many times when he thought of the house in Capernaum and his wife and children there and longed to be with them. But there was little time for looking back.

Rock of Galilee

News came that John the Baptizer had spoken out so strongly against Herod Antipas that he had been first imprisoned and then put to death. Herod's soldiers would soon be on the trail of Jesus and the twelve. Jesus decided it was best to leave Galilee and go into Trachonitis, which was under the rule of Philip, brother to Herod Antipas, but a more just ruler than his brother. The disciples, with Jesus, crossed over into Trachonitis out of the reach of Herod Antipas. They took the road to Caesarea Philippi. One morning as they sat together talking, Jesus came to them. He had been apart from them praying. Now he came and sat with them and suddenly asked, "Who do men say I am?"

"Jeremias!"

"John the Baptizer!"

"Elijah—come again, some say!"

"And who do you say I am?" asked Jesus.

"You are the Christ, the Son of the living God." The deep voice of Simon boomed out in the silence. The big man was on his feet. None of the other disciples said a word and then Simon sat down.

"Blessed are you, Simon-bar-Jonah, for no man has revealed this truth to you, but it has been revealed to you by my Father in heaven." Then Jesus talked further and gave Simon his new name, Peter—Peter, the rock on which his church would be built.

Before this Simon had been the leader of the group only through the force of his own personality and because he assumed responsibility. There were times when others of the disciples had contended with Simon for leadership of the group. James, John, and Judas had been the ones mainly to challenge Simon from time to time. Now there was no mistake. With the new name had come the formal designation by Jesus of Simon Peter as the leader of the disciples.

Slowly the disciples retraced their steps back to Capernaum. The spies of Herod were more numerous now. From Capernaum they made their way through Galilee and Samaria and into Judea. For a while they tarried at Ephraim, a village in the barren wilderness. After a while they turned east across the Jordan into Perea. Later they came back across the Jordan to Bethpage.

From Bethpage they went to Bethany, and here they visited in the home of Lazarus and Jesus performed his miracle of raising Lazarus from the tomb and restoring him to life. Many times during the last days Jesus had made reference to his own coming death. Simon Peter could not bring himself to believe that this could really happen. The fisherman had changed. He was still the impulsive, quick-spoken man who had dropped everything to follow Jesus, but these days he often sat alone and thought about what Jesus taught them. Since that day on the road to Caesarea Philippi, more than Simon's name had changed. Jesus had named him Simon Peter—Simon the rock. At first he had been bewildered, and then slowly the meaning of what Jesus had said came to him clearly.

In first one way and then another Jesus brought to Simon Peter the understanding that it would be Simon Peter's responsibility to see that Jesus' work was carried on when Jesus would no longer be with them. This was the burden Simon Peter carried inside his heart. How can I carry such a load, he thought to himself. Not only must I lose this one who has transformed my whole life, but

197

losing him I must take up his work and carry on. Once he came to Jesus to confess his own weakness.

"Lord, you say to us you must soon be taken from us. These many times with one phrase or another you have made us understand your time is soon upon you. You will leave us. You have named me Peter. Peter you have called me—the rock on which you build your church. I am a simple man, Lord. I love you truly, as you know. There is no will of yours I would not carry out, but I doubt I am the one to lead when you are gone. Would it not be better to choose John, who has a better head for understanding? If not John, then James, who is as strong-willed as I. Perhaps a better choice would be Bartholomew. You yourself recognize him for his trustworthiness. There are so many things for me to learn. Perhaps I will not have the wisdom to lead the others. You say, soon you must be taken from us. The thought of this cruel blow daily haunts my mind. But the thought of failing in the trust you give me robs me of my sleep each night. Lord, must I be the one?" Peter dropped to his knees before Jesus and his face was very troubled.

"Simon, Simon Peter. Rise and sit here beside me," Jesus said. "Don't you know I will not impose a burden too heavy for you to bear? When you took out your boat on the Sea of Galilee and lowered the net, you always made sure those whose duty it was to close the net and lift the heavy net full of struggling fish were strong enough to carry out the task. Is that not so? Then why would I choose you to lead unless I know you are equal to the task? You will make mistakes. There will be failures. But you will rise above those mistakes and conquer those failures. Believe in me, Simon Peter. Believe in me." That was the last time Jesus talked to Simon Peter in such a way. The big fisherman's heart was heavy still, but he felt comforted by what Jesus had said to him.

When the time came for them to go to Jerusalem, and the disciples walked beside Jesus as he rode into the city, Simon Peter's heart grew light again. The people cheered and threw palms on the road. Perhaps Jesus had misjudged how the people would receive him. Now there might be a change that would keep Jesus with them! But even as the thought crossed his mind, he knew this could not be. Jesus had told him he would soon be taken from them and that the hour of his suffering was not far away.

It was the day of the Passover supper. Jesus sent John and Simon Peter to arrange for a place. The two disciples went into the city and found the man bearing a pitcher of water as Jesus had told them they would. They spoke with the man and so arranged with him to use the upper room of his house and eat the Passover meal there. The events that followed were written forever in Simon Peter's memory. The Garden of Gethsemane, the watch with Jesus —even there he had failed! He had fallen asleep when Jesus had bidden him to wait and watch with him. Then came the arrival of Judas with the soldiers of the high priest. Roaring with frustration and sorrow, Peter had drawn his sword and slashed at the first soldier to approach Jesus. He slashed off the man's ear. At once Jesus had bidden him put down his sword. Quickly the soldiers surrounded Jesus and led him away.

Simon Peter followed and lingered in the courtyard of the high priest. It was there the bitterest moments of Simon Peter's whole life came up to meet him.

"You're one of them, aren't you? You're the big fellow I've seen with the Nazarene!" One of the soldiers confronted Peter in the courtyard.

"Me? I've never seen him," replied Simon Peter. But there were others about who seemed to remember him, and again the question was asked by one of the onlookers in the courtyard.

"Aren't you one of the followers of Jesus?"

"I do not know the fellow," Simon Peter said. But the question would not go away, and one of the serving maids of the high priest's household came into the courtyard and saw Simon Peter.

"You're one of the disciples who follow Jesus, aren't you?"

she asked Simon Peter. And before he could reply she said again, "You're Galilean by your accent. You must be one of them."

"Not me. I do not know him," Simon Peter hastily replied.

In the distance he heard a cock crow. The sudden remembering of Jesus' words struck him like a club. "Before the cock shall crow you'll deny me thrice."

Simon Peter rushed out of the courtyard. Now it was not for his life he cared. It was from himself he tried to run away. The big man stumbled through the early light of dawn. He had the appearance of a madman, and those who saw him drew away. On he ran. At last he came to the house where they had eaten the Passover meal. One great fist pounded on the door. Luckily the owner of the house came quickly, for no lock would have barred Simon's way for long. Rushing by the startled man, he climbed the stairs to the upper room. Simon Peter opened the door. In one corner he slumped to his knees.

"Lord, how can I carry on your work? How can I lead others when I am not worthy of your trust in me? Three times I denied you. Three times I might have testified to the living God and I denied you! I am as much your betrayer as Judas. Lord, take me with you this day." There was no end to the self-disgust and bitterness Simon Peter poured out. He was beside himself in shame at his own weakness.

There was no answer to his prayer, and from sheer exhaustion the fisherman slept. His sleep was deep, and when at last he awakened he poured out his heart again. Little by little he grew calmer. He began to recall other words of Jesus:—"There will be failures. But you will rise above those mistakes and conquer those failures. Believe in me, Simon Peter. Believe in me." Simon—Simon Peter, the rock of Galilee—rose to his feet. Slowly he left the room and walked down the stairs. He left the house and walked to Gethsemane. He would go there and perhaps he would find the courage to go on. The courage to face the other disciples.

He was tired and weak from having not eaten, but as he heard his name called he quickened his pace.

"Simon Peter, Simon Peter!" It was John calling to him. "I've been looking for you. We must find the others."

"That's what I've been thinking, John. I have so much to say to all of you. In the courtyard of Caiaphas I denied our Lord three times. Just as he said I would. I do not feel worthy to carry on his work, and yet I will! I will serve him. I'll earn the right to die for him, John. Can you look at me and still call me friend?"

"You are our leader, Simon Peter. All of us are weak. We need each other more than ever now. We can be strong together. Look who comes toward us. Isn't that Mary Magdalene?" The two disciples hurried to meet the running figure of the woman who came toward them. It was Mary Magdalene. She began speaking as soon as they came up to her.

"They have taken our Lord Jesus out of the sepulcher. We do not know where they have laid him."

John ran ahead and Simon Peter came running after him. John reached the sepulcher first and saw that the stone was rolled away. He stooped and saw through the opening the linen burial cloths lying there, but he did not go in. Now Simon Peter came up and entered the sepulcher and saw the burial cloths lying there. John followed him. Both John and Peter were puzzled and came away together to go in search of the other disciples. They left Mary Magdalene there.

Later in the day, when Simon Peter and John had assembled most of the disciples, Mary Magdalene came to them and told them she had seen Jesus and he had spoken to her.

"I waited outside the tomb not knowing what to do. Suddenly I noticed a man standing beside me. I supposed it was the gardener. I asked him if he knew where they had taken our Lord. He called me by name. He told me to go and to tell you that he ascends into heaven to be with his Father and to be with his God and our God."

For the disciples this news brought a new beginning to what many of them had regarded as the end of everything for which they dreamed. In Simon Peter especially new hope grew. Jesus had risen! The weeks that followed were weeks of deep discussion and planning among the eleven disciples. During these weeks Jesus appeared to them several times. First to all except Thomas. Later Jesus appeared again when Thomas was with them. Philip and Cleopas saw Jesus and talked with him as they walked to nearby Emmaus. New courage filled them all. As always, Simon Peter took the lead and made an important decision.

"Now we are but eleven in our company," Simon Peter said to the others as they met together. "We must choose another from among the most faithful. We must be twelve again. You recall Jesus chose twelve of us in the beginning. We must be twelve again." The others nodded their agreement.

"There are many who would join us," said James. "How will we choose?"

"Let us select two men and cast lots to decide which of the two will be our brother disciple," answered Simon Peter.

"Joseph Barsabas should be one. He is a good man," spoke up Bartholomew. The others agreed, saying Joseph should be one of the two.

"I think we should choose Matthias for the other," said Philip. "None of our followers have been more faithful than Matthias." And so these were the two decided upon, for each was equal in the eyes of the eleven. They cast lots to choose between them, and Matthias was chosen to be the new disciple.

It was now the time of Pentecost—the feast of the first fruits. The disciples came together to eat the festival meal. They were strangely stirred with a new fervor, and it seemed that the Holy Spirit came upon them. They could not describe their feelings except to speak of a great gust of wind and a vision of tongues of fire. Each man seemed to speak in languages he had never known and to hear and understand other languages, and men of all nations heard each in his own language. It was a terrifying experience for the disciples, and some of those who heard them speak of their experience mocked them and wondered if they had had too much to drink. Again it was Simon Peter who spoke for the group.

"All you men of Jerusalem listen to me. These men are not drunk. It is early in the day, as you know. This is the Spirit of the Lord which has been poured out on us." He continued on and spoke at great length, and the crowd, which had gathered to jeer them, listened. When Peter finished speaking, a large number believed what he had said. Many were baptized and began to believe in the teachings of Jesus.

The Long Road,
Gethsemane to Rome

And so the new church was coming into being. At first the Sanhedrin paid little attention to the beginnings of the new church. They had crucified Jesus. The Nazarenes, as they called the followers of Jesus, were harmless followers without a leader, so they thought. But they were wrong. Now the disciples began to move out to take the good news to other places.

For a time Simon Peter, James, and John worked primarily in Jerusalem. The Sanhedrin did take notice and imprisoned both Peter and James, but later released them. Philip went to Samaria and the others took to the dusty roads of Palestine and beyond, so the good news could spread.

Simon Peter went many places. He went to Samaria, to Joppa, to Caesarea. In Caesarea he took a great step forward by baptizing Cornelius, a Roman centurion, into the new faith. Perhaps Simon Peter went to Antioch as well. We are not sure. We know he went to Rome. As the faith grew stronger and as more people came to believe the word that was passed on, the opposition of Rome and of the high priests in Jerusalem grew strong again.

And so it was that Simon Peter, the fisherman from Galilee, turned toward Rome. He would go to Rome, to the center of the Roman Empire. He would go there to help bring the good news to the Gentiles. There in Rome would also be Paul. Paul, who was not one of the twelve but who had turned from a rabbi bitterly opposing the followers of Jesus to rank with Simon Peter as co-leader of the Christian movement.

Simon Peter traveled the road from Gethsemane to Rome through the long years. He was the same Simon Peter who had said without a second's hesitation, "You are the Christ, the Son of the living God." He was the same Simon Peter who never heard a cock crow in the early morning without feeling a knife thrust in his heart. He was older now, much older. Still tall enough and straight enough to be called the "Big Fisherman," he used a staff now when he walked. His hair was white and many of his old comrades were gone. His younger brother Andrew had died, lashed to a cross, not many years before. Long ago James had fallen by the executioner's sword in Jerusalem. Many of the others had gone. But Simon Peter and Paul and John and Matthew were still carrying on the work, and there were other, younger men now.

The church would go on no matter what happened to Simon Peter. There were enemies of the church in Rome, but his place was there. He turned his face toward Rome.

A Fisherman Comes Home

The touch on his shoulder was feather light, but the sleeping man awoke instantly. He opened his eyes wide and looked into the gusting flare of the torch held high above his head. The one who awakened him placed fingertip to mouth in a signal for silence. There was no need for the signal. Already Peter was moving quietly to prepare for a quick leave-taking. Silently he thrust his arms through the loose sleeves of the cloak which had covered him as he slept. His dark eyes looked beyond the torch. In them was the look of a man accustomed to danger. The other man spoke in a low voice.

"Sire, you must flee the city at once. Even this hiding place offers no safety. Soldiers search the city house by house. I have come to guide you to a new place where we will be safe for a time, but we *must* leave Rome."

For a few moments Peter sat on the edge of the cot lost in thought. When the catacombs, those underground meeting places and burial vaults, no longer provided safety for the Christians, Peter and some of the others had scattered to new hiding places. Still Peter had refused to leave Rome, preaching to the small groups he could muster wherever it was possible.

Lately he had made powerful enemies in Rome. Agrippa, the prefect second only to the Emperor in power, was one. Albinus, known to all of Rome as the favorite of Emperor Nero, was another. With the recent fire, started by the Emperor himself, some rumors said, the plight of the Christians had grown worse. Friends of the Emperor blamed the fire on the Christians. At last Peter rose and spoke: "Will it always be thus? Is there no place for us to do God's will and follow his teachings without persecution? How can we teach others if we must hide?" There was no fear in

Peter's voice. Anger, frustration, and sorrow perhaps, but not fear, made his voice echo from the walls of the small closed room.

"Softly, venerable sire, I beg you. Even these poor walls have ears, it seems." His companion cast a quick glance over his shoulder as if in fear some enemy might leap from the shadows beyond the circle of light cast by the torch he held.

"Yes, yes, I know, Junius. Even in my old age I've not learned to conquer impatience." Peter spoke in a lower tone as he bent painfully and secured the strap of his sandal. He picked up the heavy staff and turned to follow out the door and down the narrow passage. He carried nothing but his staff; no purse, no bundle of goods or clothing. He owned the clothes on his back, the sandals on his feet, and the staff he carried. These plus a few small coins in the pocket of his cloak—the accumulation of a lifetime. He strode the narrow passage more like a ruler than a penniless man, late in his life marked for certain death by the most powerful men in Rome.

"Where do we go, Junius? How long will it be before I can return?"

"We follow the Appian Way for a little distance and then turn to a village in the hills. A kinsman of Linus, one of our number, will keep us for a few days. Then we go south to Puteoli and arrange passage, perhaps to Antioch. As for the coming back, I fear there will be no coming back to Rome for us." Roman-born Junius spoke the words sadly. Since attaching himself to this strange band called Christians he had forsaken many of the old ways; but to give up Rome, perhaps forever, this was hard indeed.

"But there is so much for me to do here. So many people who must hear the word, so many who need to be strengthened for what may happen to us all. I do not feel it is right for me to flee. There is so much to do." Peter's rough voice gentled, almost to a whisper, as he spoke the last words again. "So much to do."

"If you stay here you will surely be taken and put to death, sire. There is no choice for you. Some are able to go unnoticed in the crowds but not you, not the one they call the Fisherman of Galilee." Junius quickened his pace.

"So that is what they call me—Fisherman of Galilee. Galilean I am and a fisherman, once. Most of us were fishermen. It's been long since I've seen Galilee. I wonder if I could still bring in a catch? How fine it would be to see the silver *mousht* wriggling in the net through the blue water. How fine it would be to go home again." The big man came to the end of the passage, still deep in his memories.

Junius turned and touched Peter's shoulder, raising his forefinger in the sign of caution. He put out the torch in a pail of water on the floor by the door. Junius placed his shoulder to the low door. Steadily he pushed. He had to use some strength to open the door, for a rude two-wheeled cart was backed against it from the outside. Old rags of cloth hung carelessly, concealing the entrance from all save searching eyes.

Gradually the door opened a crack as Junius pushed the cart a foot or two into the stable yard on which the passage opened. The way was clear. The stable yard was empty. He reached behind and touched Peter with his hand.

"Come quickly. No one is about." Junius' voice was no more than a husky whisper. He slipped through the partially opened door and held it for the older man, warning him to stoop. Peter, for all his years, moved with a quickness which did not match his white hair and beard. In a moment Junius had pushed the cart back in place.

It was early dark and the moon was not up. A good time to travel. Darkness was a friend to them now. "You must stoop over and lean on me a little. Use the staff on your other side. This way it will seem natural for you to keep your head down. You'll not appear to be so tall." Junius, shorter by a head than Peter, stood on tiptoe to whisper in the taller man's ear.

"I'll not steal away like a beggar, whimpering and limping in the dark! No matter the outcome! I'll walk on my own feet as I've done these many years." Peter grasped his staff and rammed it into the earth of the stable yard.

"Sire, you are the leader and I but a humble follower. Still, what I ask you to do is no dishonor. I have been charged by the elders of the company to see you safely from the city. This is their plan. If you will not follow it, I must do as you wish. We are few and many of us still uncertain. We need you to show us the way." Junius faced his superior without backing away. Peter's better judgment prevailed.

"Come, Junius, give me your arm. I'll try to play the feeble wretch you wish to make me out." Peter put his left arm about the younger man and dropped his head. The two of them moved slowly into the dark night away from the stable yard. This was one of the poorest sections of Rome and there were few people about. No man lingered in this section of the city after dark. He might be set upon and robbed or even killed. Here, as in many other parts, there were still blackened ruins of buildings all about. Reminders of the great fire which had occurred so recently. This area was one where the fire had raged fiercest. The two poorly dressed travelers made their way down quiet streets and dark alleys.

It was a slow pace, and occasionally they stopped while Junius went ahead to scout the way. They were in the southwestern quarter of the city, moving south and east in a roundabout way. Junius had been born, and had lived most of his life, in this section of Rome. He knew every cobblestone in every street. It was here, only a year ago, he had first heard of the strange group called Christians. They taught a way of life ruled by love, of concern for others. If one had more than he needed, he freely shared with his neighbor who had less. They spoke of the one true God to whom all things were possible, and of his son Jesus, the Messias, who lived among men. It was said that some of the leaders had actually known him. Junius understood little of what he had heard, but he was eager to know more.

Not entirely by chance, for few things happened entirely by chance to Junius Lucullus, he had encountered an elder of the group and engaged him in conversation. All his life Junius had lived by his wits. For him life was a desperate game where taking advantage of someone else was the surest way to a full stomach. There would certainly be easy pickings for a sharp mind among these simple fellows. Yet somehow it had not worked out that way. How could you rob those who freely shared whatever they had? But, most curious of all, though they had little, they were always happy!

Like a skittish colt Junius gradually became accustomed to the simple honesty of these men and women who asked only the opportunity to tell the good news which had been brought to them. Then at last this one had come, this one they called Peter. Junius had been drawn to him at once. Peter had actually known the one they called Jesus. Junius did not understand, but he almost believed the things Peter told him about Jesus and how all men were brothers and equal in the sight of God. One thing certain, this Peter had no fear in him. Some, not of the company of Christians, called him the Fisherman of Galilee and sneered at his preachings. Then the great fire had occurred which burned so much of Rome. Someone had to be blamed. There were those who wished to place the blame upon the Christians. The persecution of the Christians increased, and to be a Christian was to live in constant danger.

With something of a start Junius collected his thoughts. He would need to be especially alert from here on. They were nearing the gate that would take them out of the city and onto the Appian Way. This was the night they had to leave. The officer in charge of the gate was the brother of a centurion Peter had once befriended years ago in a place called Caesarea. This centurion would ask no questions as the two passed through the gate, accepting the simple explanation Junius gave. Junius stopped. Patrols would be about this area. They would need to take advantage of every shadow and cover available. Just ahead was a narrow, winding way lined on either side by the high walls of the *insulae*—those tenement dwellings rising four stories—where many Romans lived. This way was a favorite spot for thieves and robbers. Junius knew it well. There were no passersby and the two of them seemed poor enough to be little attraction for robbers. He would chance it! This route was shorter and would get them to the gate they sought sooner than the main streets.

Down the winding way they went. The moon, now rising, could not reach between the high walls of the narrow passage. Only a bundle of discarded rags intruded on the shadow of the building they passed. Junius' keen eyes flicked over it and passed on. He did not look back. If he had, he might have detected the slightest of movements from the bundle of rags. It might have been the stirring of the wind.

"A little more and we'll be free of the city." Junius spoke to Peter in a low voice.

"You were trying to find the key to it all, Junius? Am I right?" Peter smiled to himself in the darkness, certain he had guessed the reason for his companion's long silence.

"I was thinking about all you and the others told me. About the one you call the Messias. Tell me, this Jesus of Nazareth you talk about so much—was he born poor, as poor as I?" Junius asked the question hesitantly. Perhaps it was forbidden to ask such a question. The big man at his side could become very angry when he lost his temper.

"Born in a stable in Bethlehem. That's in Judea, far south of my home in Galilee. Born in a stable, Junius. His earthly father was a carpenter. They had enough to put on the table but not

210

much more. Is that poor? I never thought of it one way or the other. What is poor, Junius? There was a time when I had more than just enough. It was a long time ago. Then I left the sea and the boats I had always known. From that time on my bread has come to me because of someone else's generosity, and yet I've never been richer." Peter cast aside the pretense of leaning on Junius and was striding along thinking only of the conversation with his friend.

"Being poor in Rome—my kind of poor—is having neither father nor mother. Never remembering who they might have been or under which mule cart you were born. That's the kind of beginning I had," replied Junius.

"Now you have the same Father all of us have," answered Peter, putting his arm around Junius' shoulder. "God is our Father and he cares for us all. He knows us all and he watches over us."

"I believe the words you tell me, for I have learned to trust you as I have trusted no other man. If only I could *feel those words inside me,* the way I know you do." Junius was not whispering now. He had forgotten everything but the need to find a deeper meaning in these words he had learned to believe but not to really understand.

"Have the patience I too rarely have. There will come a time— perhaps soon, perhaps later—but the time will come when you feel the truth of our Lord inside you, Junius. The time will come." As always Peter spoke with sure confidence. They approached the Appian gate and Peter resumed the guise of a feeble old man leaning on the shoulder of Junius.

The centurion in charge of the group of soldiers stationed at the gate waved his fellows aside and stepped up as Junius and Peter halted before him.

"I take my old grandfather home to my father in the next village. He is not well and would see his only son before he dies." Junius did the talking. Peter was silent.

The centurion nodded to Junius and touched Peter on the arm. In a low voice he spoke to Peter. "The words spoken in Caesarea are remembered in Rome, old one. My brother has written to me of you. Make what haste you can. I can do no more than this." The centurion straightened and spoke loudly so that his comrades could hear. "Pass on."

They were on the cemented stone blocks of the Appian Way heading south from Rome, moving as rapidly as they could away from the walls of the city.

"I still feel it is wrong for me to leave Rome," said Peter, shaking his head slowly.

"Surely you do not understand, teacher. The prefect Agrippa is your sworn enemy. To make it worse, Albinus, the favorite of the Emperor, has said you must die. This means the cross! Did you not know that?" Junius looked up at Peter.

"So I've been told. I only pray I may be worthy of a death like that." Peter was smiling again.

Junius beckoned and led his companion off the Appian Way to a small tree a few yards below. They rested there. "Worthy! Of so mean a way to die? Robbers and slaves die on the cross! Only the worst of men die thus! The ancients tell the old, old story of the slaves' revolt when more than six thousand slaves hung on crosses along this Appian Way." There was amazement in Junius' voice.

Peter's eyes blazed. His voice cracked like a whip. "Do not speak to me of robbers and slaves in your ignorance. There was one who died on the cross for us all. It was no shameful death! He changed it all! A man could pray a lifetime for the right to die like him. I am not worthy. Better they place my head to the ground if I earn the cross."

Junius had started back, holding his hands in front of him, as Peter's words lashed out at him. Peter reached out to touch Junius in a gesture of conciliation, but the wary Roman sprang out of reach. His temper gone as quickly as it had come, the big man spoke gently.

"Forgive me, Junius. There is much I have not yet told you. I meant no harm. Come, let us go on." Together they walked the road. Suddenly Junius knelt and placed his ear to the ground. Peter did likewise. Junius spoke.

"I hear hoofbeats. Let us get off the road. Yonder is a thicket where we can watch unseen. We'll see who passes." Quickly the two men scrambled off the road and down to the thicket Junius had spotted some yards away. They waited, forcing themselves to breathe easily and quietly.

Peter exclaimed in disgust, "My staff! I laid my staff on the side of the road when we knelt to listen. We left so quickly I forgot to pick it up. Will it betray us?"

"Perhaps it will not be noticed." Junius hoped his words sounded braver than he felt. The moon had climbed higher now, spilling its light over the road above them. Junius could see the staff Peter had dropped. One end lay in the road. It was clearly visible.

The hoofbeats grew louder. Junius made a decision. Drawing closer to Peter he whispered hasty instructions: "After I am gone, follow the footpath along this side of the road for a few miles, perhaps three. Turn left among the ruined trees of an abandoned olive grove and cross the hill. On the other side of the hill is the village we seek. Ask for Marius. He is the kinsman of Linus. Tell him Linus sent you. Wait until I come. I go now to lead astray those who follow. The clink of metal in the distance tells me it is soldiers who come. They may seek you, but certainly they do not know me." With a bound Junius was gone before Peter could utter a word.

Peter watched as the slightly built Roman darted into the moonlight and ran to the road. In a moment he had picked up the heavy staff and was moving down the road. He was limping, pretending to be lame, when four mounted soldiers came in sight.

213

Ahead of them ran a man dressed in rags. Head lowered, the running man kept his eyes fixed on the road ahead. As he spied Junius he picked up speed. The soldiers walked their horses leisurely behind him.

Junius limped ahead without looking back. He paid no attention to the commotion behind. Suddenly the running man caught up with him. The runner placed his hand on Junius' shoulder and whirled him around.

"This is the one I saw walking with the old one earlier," he cried. "This is the one I followed. Ask him where the other one is. He's the one they call Peter. Fisherman of Galilee, some call him."

The soldiers reined in their horses. The leader of the group addressed Junius. "If you know where the one called Peter is, tell us, and do so quickly."

"I know no person called Peter. I am a Roman citizen, Junius Lucullus by name. I go seeking work among the farmers nearby."

The ragged runner, who had led the soldiers, fairly danced with anger at the thought of getting no reward for his night's work. He could hardly get the words out fast enough. "He was with the tall old one this night. He's one of them! I saw them together some two hours past. Make him tell where the other one is."

The leader of the soldiers dismounted, flinging his reins to his nearest fellow. "Junius Lucullus, you are abroad early for a man seeking honest labor. What can a lame man do in the fields to earn a wage? I'll warrant those hands never grasped scythe or pruning hook!"

With a quick tug the informer, darting beside the soldier, tore the staff from the hands of Junius. "He's not lame. This is the staff the old one carried! He's probably hiding in the city and sent this one on ahead to lead us a chase. This fellow's no farmer. He's like me. The alleys of Rome are his home."

"Play no games with me, small man. Where is the one we seek, this Peter, leader of the Christians?" The soldier placed his arm under Junius' chin and lifted his face so the smaller man could not turn away.

"I do not know where he is. Far away, perhaps. I do not know!" Junius shouted the answer at the top of his voice, hoping that Peter would hear and heed the warning.

"So that's the way it is to be." Almost regretfully the soldier mounted his horse and barked an order. A second soldier dismounted and, carrying a long length of rope, approached Junius. He tied Junius' hands behind his back and, holding the other end of the rope, remounted and moved to the head of the column. Junius trotted ahead. His ragged betrayer ran beside him shouting taunts. He was sure he would soon collect the reward he sought.

Alone in the thicket, Peter heard only the last warning words Junius had shouted. It was clear the soldiers had sought him and had taken Junius with the intent of forcing Junius to tell where Peter was. Perhaps it was best to go on as Junius had advised. Junius was a quick-witted fellow, sure to find a way out of his predicament. There was nothing Peter could do to help. He started down the path. It seemed strange without his staff. He missed it. The staff had been his companion on so many journeys. A tough piece of wood, like the oak tree from which it had come. Suddenly Peter stopped. He was shaken, almost in a daze. It was as if he were seeing something again which had happened many years ago, here on this winding footpath where the moonlight cut through the trees. It was long before dawn, but in his mind he heard a cock crow.

The blood surged to his cheeks. Peter turned around. The moonlight seemed brighter than day. Everything was clear to him now. He started running as fast as he could run. The tears in his eyes blurred his sight, but still he ran, toward the soldiers, toward Junius, toward Rome!

Junius was cheerful enough, though weary and somewhat frightened. As the soldiers walked their horses, Junius slowed his pace and caught his second wind. Surely Peter had heard his warning. He was certain he had shouted loud enough for him to hear. Marius would help Peter on his way. As for himself, Junius knew he was headed for a prison cell. It wouldn't be his first visit to a prison cell, but never for such a cause as this one. He began to feel comforted somehow. Here he was, trotting off to prison at the end of a rope. He should have been miserable. And yet he was smiling. The Fisherman was safe!

Peter's determination did not falter. It was his legs that failed him. He could run no farther without rest. He stopped. After a brief rest he was on his way again. Running and resting, running and resting, he made his way toward Rome. The moon left the sky. There were no tears in his eyes now. Only the clear resolve in his heart made his eyes seem brighter than usual.

Sometime later, just as the sun came up, he pushed his way through the gate hidden in a crowd of peddlers bound for the city to sell their wares. He made for the center of the city. Old legs could run no more—but they could walk. That staff would be a welcome help just now. Toward him came a sight he welcomed—an armed maniple of soldiers. Peter stopped in the middle of the street and waved his arms.

"I am Peter, called by some of you the Fisherman of Galilee. I am told you seek me. Here I am. Do with me what you will." Peter dropped his hands to his side.

The soldier Peter addressed turned to another. "Caius, this is the fellow Marcus was speaking of an hour ago. Remember he brought in one of his followers? Go ahead and tell Marcus we bring the leader of the Christians to Mamertine prison." The other soldiers closed ranks around Peter. They marched behind the rapidly disappearing figure of the one called Caius.

The march was not long. Before they reached the prison the centurion Marcus came hurrying to meet them. "So this is the one," he said, looking at Peter. "Why did you give yourself up? We've gotten precious little out of your follower, Junius. We would have had to use sterner measures soon. He'll be glad to keep his skin on his back. Though little good it may do him."

Peter simply smiled and shook his head. He was too weary to talk. They placed him in a cell and he heard a sudden gasp. It was too dark for him to make out who his cellmate might be. Slowly his eyes adjusted to the dark. Now he could see Junius standing before him, the tears running down his cheeks.

"Don't grieve, Junius. You are a brave man. You gave yourself up to save me."

"For nothing! It amounted to nothing! They caught you anyway. For the first time in my life I felt really happy. In prison, and I felt happy! I wasn't even afraid. All for nothing!" Junius sank to his knees, his head in his hands.

Peter knelt beside him. "It was not a useless sacrifice, Junius. They didn't catch me. I came back to give myself up. Don't you see, I couldn't let someone suffer in my place—not again! And yet I almost did! After you were taken by the soldiers, I went on toward the village. Then the true meaning of what I was doing came over me and I turned back toward Rome."

"I don't understand." Junius turned his face up toward Peter. "You will," said Peter. "There is a part of the story I haven't told you. I hope they will let you go soon. I am so tired I can scarcely keep awake. Let me sleep a little while and I'll tell you all about it." Making a pillow of his cloak, Peter slept.

The weeks had passed slowly alone in his cell. Often Peter wondered what had happened to Junius. The street boy of Rome who had found his first real happiness in a prison cell—Peter thought of him often. He had pleaded for the boy, but his jailors would tell him nothing of what had happened. They had had the

217

one night together, and Peter had told Junius all that had happened long ago on that night in Gethsemane and the next morning. He spared nothing of his own denial. The next morning Junius had been taken away.

For himself Peter knew the days were coming to a close. He could sense it in the way the guards looked at him when they brought his meager meals. At first they had talked to him freely, but lately the conversation had stopped. Outside the cell he heard the tramp of marching feet. More than the one usual guard was coming! The door to his cell opened. The captain of the guard beckoned and spoke but a single word. "Come."

Peter walked toward him and through the open door of his cell. "It is the time I have waited for?"

"It is that time," came the answer.

"Have they granted my request?" asked Peter.

"They've done that, though we've never had a stranger one!" The captain looked at Peter with a curious respect.

Down the passage they walked. Peter thought for a moment of his home country and the blue water he had loved. Galilee had never seemed closer. He heard a voice cry out and turned his head to hear.

"Teacher, it is I, Junius." The voice came from the cell Peter was passing. Through the wide iron bars he could just see the dim form of his old companion.

"Junius! I hoped they had released you! They wouldn't tell me what had become of you." There was both gladness and sorrow in Peter's greeting.

"I've been here all the time. I wanted to tell you. I understand now! I truly understand! That's all that matters. I feel it inside me. Now I know why you came back. You promised someday I'd understand. Do you remember?" Junius' voice was strong and happy.

"I remember, Junius. I remember. It was you who helped me

to remember so many things. Good-bye, Junius." The guards urged Peter on.

The small group stepped into the sunlight. The sun was high. Long shadows cast strange crossed patterns on the hard-baked clay. The sky was blue—blue as a lake in Galilee.

SOURCES

Avi-Yonah, Michael, and Kraeling, Emil G. *Our Living Bible*. New York. McGraw-Hill, 1962

Bacon, D. F. *Lives of the Apostles of Jesus Christ*. 1846.

Bailey, Albert E. *Jesus and His Teachings*. Philadelphia: Christian Education Press, 1942.

Barclay, William. *The Master's Men*. Nashville: Abingdon Press, 1959.

Berdyaev, Nicholas. *The Meaning of History*. New York: Scribner's, 1936.

Brown, Charles Reynolds. *These Twelve: A Study in Temperament*. New York: Century Co., 1936.

Cave, W. *Cave's Lives of the Apostles*. Oxford University Press, 1840.

Duckat, Walter, *Beggar to King*. New York: Doubleday, 1968; Apex edition, Nashville: Abingdon Press, 1971.

Glover, Carl A. *With the Twelve*. Nashville: Cokesbury Press, 1939.

Greenhough, J. G. *The Apostles of Our Lord*. London: A. C. Armstrong & Son, *ca.* 1904.

Kent, Charles Foster. *Bible Geography and History*. New York: Scribner's, 1911.

Keyes, Nelson Beecher. *Story of the Bible World*. Maplewood, N.J.: C. S. Hammond, 1959.

Kraeling, Emil G. *The Disciples*. Chicago: Rand McNally, 1967.

SOURCES

Magary, Alvin E. *Saints Without Halos.* Nashville: Abingdon Press, 1951.

Mygatt, Tracy Dickinson, and Witherspoon, Frances. *The Glorious Company.* New York: Harcourt, Brace, 1928.

Parmelee, Alice. *They Beheld His Glory.* New York: Harper & Row, 1967.

Pax, W. E. *In the Footsteps of Jesus.* New York: Putnam's, 1970.

Pittenger, W. Norman. *The Life of Saint Peter.* New York: Franklin Watts, 1971.

Robertson, A. T. *Epochs in the Life of Simon Peter.* New York: Scribner's, 1934.

Walsh, William Thomas. *St. Peter the Apostle.* New York: Macmillan, 1948.

Atlas of the Bible, ed. L. H. Grollenberg. New York: Thomas Nelson, 1957.

The Golden Bible Atlas, Samuel Terrien. New York: Golden Press, 1957.

The New Atlas of the Bible, Jan H. Negenman. New York: Doubleday, 1969.

Rand McNally Atlas of the Bible, ed. Emil G. Kraeling. Chicago: Rand McNally, 1956.

The New Westminster Dictionary of the Bible, ed. Henry S. Gehman. Philadelphia: Westminster Press, 1970.

The Interpreter's Dictionary of the Bible, ed. George A. Buttrick. Nashville: Abingdon Press, 1962.

The Interpreter's One-Volume Commentary on the Bible, ed. Charles M. Laymon. Nashville: Abingdon Press, 1971.

The New English Bible

The Revised Standard Version of the Bible

The Jerusalem Bible

The King James Version of the Bible